painting
IN THE
dark

painting
IN THE
dark

THE LONGING TO BE SEEN, TO BE HEARD, TO BE KNOWN

paul thorson

INTEGRITY®
PUBLISHERS
Nashville

Published by Integrity Publishers, a division of Integrity Media, Inc., 5250 Virginia Way, Suite 110, Brentwood, TN 37027.

HELPING PEOPLE WORLDWIDE EXPERIENCE *the* MANIFEST PRESENCE *of* GOD.

Cover Design: Roy Roper, wideyedesign
Cover Photo: Getty Images
Interior Design: Sharon Collins, Artichoke Design

Library of Congress Cataloging-in-Publication Data
Thorson, Paul.
  Painting in the dark / Paul Thorson.
     p. cm.
  Summary: "Escaping the performance trap to find a new sense of self, and a new sense of God"--Provided by publisher.

  ISBN-13: 9-781-59145-427-4
  ISBN-10: 1-59145-427-1 (pbk.)

  1. Christian life. I. Title.
  BV4501.3.T477 2006
  248.4--dc22

                              2005036459

Printed in the United States of America
06 07 08 09 10 VP 9 8 7 6 5 4 3 2 1

To the One—You continue to love me to Yourself. . . .

table of contents

acknowledgments

Thanks to Michael Blanton for years of believing in me as a teacher and now as an author. I am grateful also for Integrity Publishers and Byron Williamson for encouraging me and giving this book room to breathe.

I have been blessed with a wonderful editor in Elisa Stanford; thanks for your artistry and patience in our first "Painting."

My dear friends from *Joyful Hearts*, you have taught me much of what I'm writing and supported us in so many ways. Thanks.

To our Kiev brothers and sisters at *Bozhy Dotyk* Church ("God's Touch"), we love you. *Slava Bogu!* Thanks to Yulia Zhmurko for listening to God and letting Him speak through you into our lives.

To *Campus Crusade*, thanks for being the womb through which God birthed me. *World Harvest Mission*, thanks for all I'm continuing to learn through *Sonship*.

To Bruce and Steve, I couldn't have better brothers. We are together a testimony of God's faithfulness to Mom and Dad.

To Jon, Marty and Nat, I am and will always be most proud to be your father.

And finally to my wife, Gail, you are still my dream. Thank you for being more than I could ask or imagine.

an introduction

A couple of years ago, I began writing a novel. As preparation for this I read a how-to book describing the most important elements of a good novel. The author wrote about how important "conflict" was to a good story. She recommended writers imagine that in the first scene the hero is being chased by some danger and climbs a tree to safety. He or she mutters a sigh of relief, only to notice the enemy gathering a supply of rocks at the foot of the tree.

The author said that from that point on, a good novelist will have the enemy throwing rocks at the hero in every scene. We will read with fascination and anticipation, wondering how the hero will be saved.

Tension and release—the stuff of a good song, play, novel, or *life*! Our reality is filled with many scenes like that, a lot of tension and some release.

I have a good friend, a big guy, maybe six feet five or so. Brad told me how, after hearing one of my talks about this, he drove home, climbed a tree in his backyard, and began yelling at God! He needed help; he wanted answers to hard questions.

I'm sure his wife must have thought he'd lost it. If my friend Howard and I had known about it, I have no doubt that our idea of helping Brad would have been to sneak into the yard and shoot a video of our tall friend sitting up in that tree, yelling at someone nobody could see. (With friends like that. . . .) But Brad was the hero running from danger, and he ran to the right place.

This book is about rocks being lobbed at people like you and me who have climbed some tree somewhere looking for safety. It is about the process of letting go of the need to build and sustain the reputation we use to protect ourselves. It is about discovering that on our best days we are weaker than we ever knew and more loved than we ever hoped.

◊ ◊ ◊

So here we are, up a tree, yelling at someone nobody can see, and it is exactly the right place to begin our story. . . .

*"The One
had no
audience,
no need
for an
audience."*

CHAPTER 1

a performance

I had a great seat.

It was the Aspen Music Festival held each summer in the spectacular Rocky Mountains of Aspen, Colorado. This was called the Juilliard of the West, named for the famous music conservatory in New York. The finest classical student musicians came to study and play under the tutelage of the world's finest teachers and musicians. Each afternoon a huge blue-and-white striped tent, set up around a permanent stage, was the site of a variety of concerts. I was a guest, not a participant, of the festival.

This particular day was special. A year-long competition had been held to find the best young violinist in the world. Part of the prize for winning this competition included a chance to perform with the Aspen Chamber Orchestra. And today was the day. This year an eighteen-year-old man from Canada had been chosen as the best young violinist.

Did I mention I had a great seat? Not in the center section where you'd expect it. No. For this particular concert

I was seated way over on the left side of the audience facing the orchestra. I could actually see backstage behind the orchestra from my seat. Not ideal for listening, but on this day it was the most interesting place to be.

I don't remember which violin concerto they played. I do remember that the orchestra, under the leadership of Juilliard conductor Jorge Mester, was terrific. When the young violinist began his solo, it was evident why he had been chosen. He had wonderful talent. The audience was enthralled with the performance—until, suddenly, the young man stopped playing. The orchestra continued but it was obvious something was wrong. The conductor's baton flashed as he cut off the orchestra in mid-phrase and gestured to the young violinist to come over to the podium. The eighteen-year-old prodigy had forgotten his solo.

The young man reluctantly stepped over to look at the conductor's score, then returned to his place to the conductor's left. Mester began the concert where they had prematurely ended. Two minutes later, the young man again stopped playing. The audience held its breath. As before, he was invited to look at the conductor's score to remind himself of what he was supposed to be playing.

Remember, the committee who had selected this winner of the competition had eliminated hundreds of other outstanding violinists to arrive at their choice. He was every bit a great violinist, but today of all days, he was struggling mightily.

Once more, the orchestra began. The young Canadian played, and within minutes, you can guess what happened. Yes, he forgot his music yet again. This time, in complete disgust, without looking back, he turned—violin and bow in hand—and hurried around the orchestra, heading for a door backstage that led off to a dressing room.

But he wasn't alone.

The conductor immediately stopped the concerto, stepped down from his podium, and followed the violinist step for step around the orchestra. Both individuals disappeared through the back door. The audience was stunned. I was stunned.

This, by the way, was an audience of musicians. Of all the audiences you most want to impress, of all the audiences you most want to play your best for, this was it. In front of this audience, this award-winning violinist was experiencing the worst meltdown of his young career.

The audience seemed to understand the feelings of this violinist, his frustration and embarrassment. Perhaps because of their own personal experiences, they knew what he must be agonizing through. They began to clap. Not randomly, but as one voice, rhythmically. (What else would you expect from a group of musicians?) *Clap, clap.* The orchestra, unable to clap because of the instruments they were holding, began to stomp their feet in unison with the clapping. The stomping echoed from under the risers on which they were seated. *Stomp, stomp, clap, clap* . . . as though synchronized thunder strokes from heaven.

Did I mention I had a great seat?

I watched as the backstage door opened, light poured out into the darkness behind the orchestra, and the young violinist stumbled over the threshold. He had, in fact, been *pushed* out the door by his grim-faced conductor! The conductor proceeded to prod the young prodigy-turned-prodigal with his baton around the orchestra and back to the place of honor where he had begun this disastrous concert.

Not surprising, the violinist had forgotten his violin and bow, which may have been lying in pieces somewhere behind that backstage door. One of the orchestra's violinists graciously offered his instrument to the humiliated soloist. The conductor raised his baton and the concert began again—its fourth beginning, and its last. This time there was no forgetting and the concert ended with a standing ovation.

◊ ◊ ◊

Sometimes, worse things can happen to you than losing a chance to perform for a great audience. You could win, and then self-destruct!

How do you think this violinist felt about his performance? A better question: how do you think he felt about himself? For many of us, it is impossible to distinguish between the two.

My guess is that he wished the stage would open up and swallow him. He wished this particular audience would have no memory of him. He wished they would never see him again and he would never see them.

How difficult it is for performers to separate their performance from their identity as a person. Ask most people, "Who are you?" and they might say, "I'm a teacher" or "I'm an engineer." But what is the *truest* thing about you? If you are an eighteen-year-old violinist who has just suffered through the worst experience of your life, who are you?

I am a failure.

Do you run and hide?

Yes, of course.

That's normal. Get drunk and try to forget it ever happened?

Why not?

That's one temporary solution that probably sounds pretty good at the moment.

If performance is what I do, and identity is who I am, reputation is others' interpretation of my performance and identity. Whatever my reputation in the world is, it's seen through someone else's eyes, not my own. I have some measure of control over my performance and identity, but not much control over how others choose to see me. Yet I find that my pursuit of reputation—the one thing I have little control over—consumes me. I perform so others notice me and what others think of my performance becomes my *raison d'être*. If I cannot perform, what is the reason for my existence?

Artists, actors, musicians, and writers are known for their fragile egos. Why not? We put our creations on display for the world to see. We live in extremes, inviting criticism as surely as we invite praise and feeling both, often in the same breath. Still, how often we forget the applause of the audience and remember only that one guy who left early. We can only speculate as to why. And we do.

Little wonder so many of us run and hide behind various addictions and depressions. Who we are seems inextricably bound to our performance as we build our identity on the sinkhole of public opinion. Our performance never ends.

Don't stop there. You don't need to be an artist to be a performer. Many of us live to build our reputation, and though the building is never completed, we list it on the market and wait desperately for someone to buy it.

But life works against me. I can't be perfect in every relationship. Often I blurt out something that tears a friend down and he thinks less of me for saying it. Who can blame him? Or I break a promise and disappoint someone, making it harder for her to trust my next promise.

Sometimes someone else hurts my reputation. A business partner makes an unethical decision and my name is on the product. A child acts foolishly, bringing shame on our family, and I am embarrassed to discover that my first reaction is to be more worried about my own reputation than I am about helping my child.

It takes brutal honesty to realize this. All the while, it unsettles me to realize how little control I have over how others interpret my identity. In the face of my failures, I run to my favorite addictions, looking for a place to hide. I overdose on football games. Or I put on a movie and hope to escape into someone else's world for two hours and forget my personal disappointments. And these are just the "acceptable" addictions. What if they get worse than that?

Everybody seems to be groping in the dark for back doors. Few, if any, of our addictions deliver on their promises. None lasts long enough.

And somewhere in the confusion of our successes and our failures, each of us asks, *What is the truest thing about me?*

◊ ◊ ◊

Maybe the best way I can begin to answer that question is to remember the story of a little girl, born during the heart of the Great Depression. . . .

*"And there He
found all the
reasons He
could ever
need to love
the many."*

a little girl

the was born into a traditional Scandinavian immigrant family, the middle child surrounded by nine brothers and sisters. They lived just south of a cold northern Canadian border.

Her father was a hard-working farmer, sacrificing to provide for his family on unforgiving land. Harsh winters shortened the growing seasons. Life was serious business and he wasn't given to showing much affection.

Maybe he found it difficult to give himself equally to each of his children. What parent doesn't?

Maybe he was angry because life turned out to be severe, and returning tired from the fields each day left him with barely enough energy to go around. Ten children—that's a weighty responsibility.

For whatever reason, this little girl felt as though she somehow slipped through the cracks of that old weathered farmhouse and old weathered farmer. She felt unloved.

Perhaps it was just self-pity—of course she was loved.

Maybe it was just never enough for her. One thing was certain, there was nothing this little girl wanted more in life than to feel loved by her papa. But there was an awkwardness, not at all malicious, a kind of clumsiness in her timing. Asking questions when he was talking to someone else, wanting to jump into his arms after he'd just returned from an especially exhausting day in the fields. Too much, too soon, too little, too late, and she felt his unconscious reaction to her untimely interruptions. Knowing too well that tired rebuke she saw in his eyes, she retreated from a rejection she suspected was her own fault.

When she finished high school in their one-room schoolhouse, this little girl in a woman's body left home, moved to the big city, and found work as a secretary in a factory. It wasn't long before a handsome young sailor came into the office and charmed his way into her simple life. With promises of undying love he swept her off her feet and into his bed.

One summer evening, fearing the worst, she tearfully revealed to him that their passion had led to an unplanned pregnancy. The self-centered sailor had no interest in the responsibilities of being a father, and this relationship was about to rob him of his freedom.

He may have announced his plans; he may have even said good-bye. He packed his bags and took a Greyhound bus out of town.

What do you do when you leave home to seek love and instead find yourself all alone in a big city and pregnant, watching your first chance to be cherished trade you for the next bus out of town?

This little girl in a woman's body sat down and wrote the hardest letter of her life:

"Dear Papa, I'm pregnant . . ."

If he didn't seem willing to show love and affection to her when her only sin was poor timing, what could she possibly expect now?

"The father of my child said he wouldn't marry me and ran away. . . ."

How would she ever be able to return home after this shameful failure? How could she ever look her papa in the eyes again?

"Can you forgive me for what I've done . . . ?"

She mailed the letter. Then she waited. And she remembered the hymns. Her family was religious, a religion often defined by rule keeping. But she had warm memories of her mama and papa and all the children gathering around the upright piano in that old farmhouse, harmonizing together. So she cried out to the God of those old hymns, and somehow she found Him. She believed and she asked God for forgiveness. He promised His heart to her and she felt loved.

She had barely hoped for forgiveness, so when she found love as well, she promised her heart to Jesus—a promise she kept.

Was it a phone call or a letter?

She didn't say.

Maybe she opened her mailbox one day, her hand shaking as she pulled out the letter from her papa. She cried as she read: *"Dear Daughter, I'm so sorry. . . ."*

No shame. Just compassion.

"Yes, I forgive you. . . ." She wasn't forgotten; she wasn't exiled for her sin. She felt loved by her papa.

"I'm sending your older brother to visit you, and he will take you, and together you will find this father of your child and talk to him about his responsibility. . . ." That's what they

did in those days. She felt cared for. More than that, she felt like someone was defending her. She thanked God.

They found the sailor some five hundred miles south, working as a taxi driver and scared. Confronted by his pregnant girlfriend and her no-nonsense big brother, he agreed to marry her.

Not exactly a "match made in heaven." Not the way she dreamt it would be, and the pain wasn't over. She soon discovered that this young man was not only selfish and afraid, he was also an alcoholic. So this young girl in a woman's body married a reluctant husband, an immature father, and an alcoholic.

What a prize.

She assumed that this was part of the consequence of her choices. If life on the farm had taught her anything, it had taught her that life, on its best days, was hard work. So she suffered in private. She prayed a lot. And cried a lot.

When her little boy was born, she was so happy, and so thankful, and so confused. He was the product of her recklessness. But he was beautiful. He was conceived out of weakness, but she couldn't kiss him enough. And the questions poured out of her. . . .

How could he be a gift from God? But he was!

How could she ever have hoped he might not be born? But she had.

Two lovers, in a moment of uncontrolled passion, and now this baby in her arms, with his papa's blue eyes and his mother's smile. And she couldn't stop crying, and she loved him, and she was afraid.

Should she be proud of the child or embarrassed? She felt both and was ashamed.

Six months after her son was born she found herself

pregnant again. Nine months later she gave birth to a second son and eighteen months later, a third son. She loved her family but couldn't shake her fears.

She was being accused by voices in her head, voices that wouldn't go away. They told her that her firstborn son was not a gift from God but only the result of her carelessness. They said, *"Don't be surprised if he turns out bad."* Most parents dream about what their children will become. She was having nightmares. She worried and she prayed.

The story of this mother is the beginning of my story, for I was her firstborn little boy.

◊ ◊ ◊

Experts say that a baby can feel the emotional tides that ebb and flow in the womb of his or her mother. I don't know about that—I mean I don't doubt that it may be true; I just don't know about it for me. For years I was unaware of the circumstances surrounding my conception. I didn't bother to figure out that my birthday came sooner than it should have after my folks' wedding anniversary, which seemed to come and go without much fanfare.

One day Mom took me aside in our midwestern kitchen and told me the truth. I was fourteen or fifteen years old. Maybe she thought I would discover the truth on my own. Maybe she watched me stumbling into adolescence and thought I needed a severe warning about hormones. She was uncharacteristically nervous and obviously ashamed, but I brushed it aside as though it didn't matter.

But it did. More than I knew.

Now, I am famous in our home today for not noticing things. My wife, Gail, and I have three sons, and our youngest son, Nat, teases me, calling me Mr. No Notice.

He's right too. But on that particular day I remember standing in the doorway between the kitchen and the living room, shifting from foot to foot, staring at the divider between the rooms, a three-foot-high wall that shelved cups and saucers, odds and ends, and piled-up photographs. I remember the difficulty my mom had making eye contact with me. How do I remember such detail when I don't even know what color my socks are today?

It wasn't until about twenty-five years later that I began to suspect a profound reality. It always seemed to be about me when there were problems with us boys—even when we had grown to men. My wife said she saw this from the first time she watched all of us interact together.

Of course, I earned my share of the discipline as a child, but more was going on than my anger and willfulness. Mom carried so much unnecessary guilt; she believed the voices that told her, *"Your failure will lead to his failure."* She was determined to keep me in line and protect me from my fate.

And the law fell hard on the firstborn.

Unknowingly, she passed on that fear of consequence to me. I, too, expected to fall someday, bringing shame on myself and my family. Growing up, I didn't understand where that expectation came from, but it haunted me. I had been sentenced to inevitable failure. My crime? Being born.

How does a kid dig himself out of a hole like that? By doing what I did. By becoming a performer! A show-off.

I realize, looking back, that I had set out to prove it was okay I had been born. Those things I did well, I boasted about. How else was anyone going to know? They would never realize how much was at stake in my being recognized and valued.

I wasn't performing for their applause and praise—their

praise could never be enough. *I was performing for the right to exist.* It wore the trappings of reputation building, but it felt more like survival.

What was the truest thing about me? One thing drove me more than any other: the need to know I was wanted and loved.

◊ ◊ ◊

Show-offs all have one thing in common: they must have an audience. Without people watching, their performance is pointless.

Years after I discovered my past, I sat down with a counselor, the late Dr. Jack Miller, founder of World Harvest Mission. I told him about my struggle, and he responded, "You have too big an audience." He was right. My audience was enormous, and always growing. I added nearly everyone I met!

Every person I wanted to impress became part of my audience. Each one might be the one who would once and for all validate me: *"You are not an accident."* Perhaps Dr. Miller realized that I moved him into the front row.

By now someone might be thinking, *Come on, Paul, deal with it. Life is tough for everyone; this self-pity is sick stuff.* Of course you are right, and those of us stuck in self-pity wish we could just "deal with it." We are angry, sometimes for good reasons. We are afraid and we are alone. Let me explain.

Somewhere in childhood, I unconsciously divided my audience into two groups: those who liked me and wanted my friendship, or those who were at best hostile, at worst indifferent, to me. (Performers would rather be hated than ignored.)

At the beginning, it didn't appear so systematic, but as I grew up, the system became more developed. I didn't trust those who liked me, but I seemed able to trust those who didn't like me.

This may seem contradictory, but I assumed that those who liked me must not be able to see me for who I really was. Those who rejected me had seen the real me and responded reasonably, pulling away.

Those who liked me I almost disdained. *Aren't they smart enough to realize I'm predestined for disaster? Are they so desperate for friends?*

Those who didn't like me I feared, even though I believed them. *What if they expose me, blow my cover? They know the truth about me.*

Little wonder I was so alone. I was running away from half my audience, and the other half was running away from me. What bad luck! A performer with no possibility of success. I was afraid and angry, trying to quiet the accusations that filled my thoughts.

◊ ◊ ◊

**But the voices that haunted my mother
were after me too. . . .**

CHAPTER 3
voices

all my life I have enjoyed being a pioneer. I love going where others seldom venture—whether blazing a trail through the woods near my grandmother's farm in Minnesota or snorkeling off the reefs of Fiji with my wife. Maybe this is why I often find myself looking for fresh ways to express familiar truths. Exploring new paths of thought has become, for me, an art form.

But I haven't always understood this about myself—and it's taken years for me to let myself be like this. Growing up in the traditional school system with traditional models of education, I was terribly out of place. I sat in class and stared out the window daydreaming about baseball and girls. Suddenly the teacher would call on me and I would dissolve in embarrassment, with no idea what the question was, much less the answer.

The system's voices labeled me *lazy*, *apathetic*, and maybe even *stupid*. I heard them loud and clear, and I believed them. It wasn't until many years later that I discovered

I had Attention Deficit Disorder, or ADD. But in those days I was just another overactive, terribly bored boy who suffered through school.

Near what should have been the end of my high school tedium, I was hanging precariously over the precipice of certain failure in my English class. Fourteen days and one as-yet-unwritten paper stood between graduation and me. I had to get an A on the paper in order to pass the class and graduate. I didn't know what an A looked like in anything but choir and PE, but I couldn't bear the thought of repeating another year.

I took a huge chance: I wrote my paper about how it felt growing up as the child of an alcoholic father.

I can't tell you what I wrote exactly, but I can tell you that I was shocked and overjoyed when I got the paper back with an A marked on it. I was going to graduate on time. I was also quietly ashamed. I had stooped to an all-time low.

Voices in my head told me I had traded on my dad's drinking problem as a way to gain pity from the teacher. That she felt sorry for me and tossed me an A, though I surely didn't deserve it.

And I believed those voices.

For many years I looked back on that experience and was convinced I had once again bluffed my way through an impossible situation. It wasn't until postgraduate studies and the help of a wise professor that I realized I had the instincts and intuition of a writer. It dawned on me, *Maybe those voices weren't true. Maybe I wasn't stupid. Maybe I was bored for good reasons. Maybe the teachers were boring.* But the voices had sounded so reasonable. After all, there was no denying I procrastinated on pretty much every deadline I ever had. But I was a writer even back then, and my

English teacher recognized some facet of that and awarded me the grade I had earned—not a grade I had manipulated her into giving.

Do you live with voices, never imagining you have permission to challenge them, to make them prove their case? For all their subtlety, these voices can be relentless. . . .

◊ ◊ ◊

Soliloquy
Voices

When?

In the in-between of night, somewhere after dark and before light, my thoughts, a slough of voices, noises too noisy to be easily missed and too often and too honest to be easily dismissed.

When will I know it's You?

From a lingering guilt haunting my regrets, and from dizzying heights of accusation I plummet, not at all a free fall.

Damned by unfinished business, and random penance, I vow midflight corrections while doubts of sincere repentance bargain for mercy.

Sleep. It seems my best escape from these voices. Voices careening down the fault lines of my overactive conscience.

Crazy? Maybe. Afraid? Absolutely.

In my waking, a false hope. Perhaps I can organize the madness and postpone the sadness and disappointment.

But potential and contentment wait still,

anxious and provocative in their teasing,
and reeling I cry, "Please. . . .

"When will I know it's You?
When will I know You are here?
In the dull and distance of uncertainty,
when will I know You still love me,
and when is that enough . . . ?"

And somehow, as long as I long to know when,
In a slough of voices, I hear You whisper,
"Now."

◊ ◊ ◊

When I ask if you have voices in your head, I'm not suggesting you've "lost it." All of us hear voices, don't we? Maybe not the kind that persuades a man like Jimmy Stewart's character to jump into a river in *It's a Wonderful Life*. I mean thoughts racing through your consciousness that sound like voices: *"I'm late again—I'm so stupid!" "I'm so ugly. No one could ever love me!"*

How do I recognize the difference between good voices and bad, true and false? Is there a difference? Some would have us believe there is not. A good friend of mine told me about the time he thought he heard a voice telling him to leave work early one afternoon and wait at a particular bus stop for someone to come by who needed to tell him something. Yeah, I know it sounds pretty vague and not a little sketchy, but my friend believed the voice, left work early, and waited for someone. No one came.

Maybe the voices whisper, *"That guy at work is jealous of me,"* or *"That girl at school never notices me."* Often, if not always, the voices speak in the first person, *"I just know that those people over there are laughing at me."* Have you noticed that the voices often shame you when you mess up? *"I can't believe I just said that. I'm so dumb!"*

The voices love to drain the hope right out of you. They love to use words like *never, always, only.* *"I never balance the checkbook. I'm always running behind. I'm the only man on the face of the earth still wearing English Leather."*

And when the voices start giving you mixed messages— that's when it really gets interesting.

"I'm a lousy artist; no one buys my work anymore."

And ten minutes later: *"I am the greatest impressionist artist since Monet. That other guy's work hanging over there—the paintings with the Sold signs on them—it's way overrated."*

I may hear a voice persuading me that it's okay to stretch the truth—*"Everyone does it"*— and then later the same voice saying, *"That was the worst thing I could have done. I'm such a liar!"*

What is the truth about me? Where do I go to learn how to distinguish the thoughts I wrestle with every day? How do I know which voices I can trust?

◊ ◊ ◊

King Solomon, the wisest man of his day, writes, "As [a man] thinks in his heart, so is he" (Proverbs 23:7 NKJV). How do I think "right" thoughts about myself in my heart and quiet the voices that rumble around in my head? How can I keep myself from allowing people who are just as insecure as I am to pass judgment as to whether or not I have value as a person? It's crazy to give others so much power over me, but I do. And the way I think about myself is often the window through which others see me. If I think I'm a loser, chances are that others will think that too.

Sometimes I seem to have only glimpses of truth, only snatches and phrases of disconnected realities. But my soul craves something or someone infinitely more satisfying.

What if who I am is not determined by others, by their reviews or opinions? What if my reputation is first of all a matter of the heart—my heart? Can someone tell me where to find a rationale for life, relationships, and me?

◊ ◊ ◊

I never expected Billy Batson to be part of my reluctant search for the truth. . . .

CHAPTER 4

Billy and me

I can still see him now. He was fairly short and very wide, hair jet black and crew cut. He was strong—scary strong—and smart.

At times his vocabulary seemed somewhat limited to words of about four letters. But I had never heard anyone so creative with those four letters. The combinations he used! What a "gift" Billy had with words.

Maybe the most memorable thing about Billy was his laugh. Perhaps you've heard somebody with an unusual laugh—it makes everyone around laugh just to hear it. At least that's how it is the first few times you hear it. After a while it might not seem so funny; it may be even annoying.

Billy had a laugh like a machine gun. Can you hear it? *Eh-eh-eh-eh-eh-eh-eh.* Just make the sounds you used to make when you were a kid playing army: *eh-eh-eh-eh-eh-eh-eh.* That's it!

Oh, did I mention that he could get angry at times? Beyond angry. Unfortunately those times always seemed to have something to do with my being present. I don't know why he hated me, but for a show-off like me, this was one tough audience.

I met Billy when I was still in college and he was already working a full-time job. High school and college summers for me and my friends usually meant working all week and playing all weekend. My dad was manager of a moving company. I worked for him for a few summers, but for various reasons, I worked for another company the rest of the time. Eight summers and many different coworkers came and went, but I can remember the name of only one of the guys I worked with: Billy Batson.

I can still hear it. The foreman walks into the warehouse, clipboard in hand, and begins to assign all the workers to their jobs for the day. I'm holding my breath, praying I won't have to spend another miserable day working with that bundle of rage.

The foreman calls out the jobs. I wait for my name. "Batson, you take Thorson and a truck to this address. . . ." I hear from somewhere in the room a string of creative curses. Billy grabs the paperwork and glares at me. "Come on!" I try to look as if I don't care, but he sees right through me.

Billy's combination of anger and disgust for me promises another ten hours of intimidation. Stuck in a smoke-filled, tension-filled truck, we drive to the home where we are supposed to unload a customer's furniture and household goods. We begin by carrying boxes filled with books or dishes inside. Later, Billy is pushing me from the opposite end of a heavy couch as we carry it into the house. The wife gestures to the wall on our left and asks us to place it there.

A few trips later, the woman waits until we've set our boxes down and says, "I wonder if you could move that couch to the opposite wall. I'm not sure I like it where it is." Billy scowls. We move it and she thanks us as we go back to the truck.

A bit later she catches us on our way out the door. "I'm so sorry to bother you, but if you don't mind, I'd like to see what the couch would look like on this other wall. . . ." I don't even want to look at Billy now. I hear him threatening under his breath and I correctly guess that he intends to take his wrath out on me.

It's only a few minutes later when the woman apologizes, "This is the last time I'll ask, but could you move the couch to its original place?"

I hurry out to the truck, but Billy is faster than I thought and I'm trapped in there when he rushes in, scorching the air with his curses. He grabs a chair and slams it across the truck, reducing it to kindling. I find the inventory sheet. Next to the item "kitchen chair" I add a note: "The legs are a little loose." And so goes another day on the job with Billy Batson.

One of the happier days in my life was the last day of my last summer working with Billy. No more fits of rage. No more disdain and rejection. And no more of his irritating machine-gun laugh. I should have walked out the door going, "*Eh-eh-eh-eh-eh-eh. . . .*"

◊ ◊ ◊

Life has a way of making you realize that you bring your own share of selfishness and foolishness into each relationship. We see that it's not always the other person who is the problem.

It happened in the middle of my first junior year of university. Studying was a low priority for me in those days. I was invited to a concert, and being a music major, I was interested. The group was definitely better than I expected (later that year they won a Grammy), but the real surprise was all the members of this band were Christians.

My parents had taken me to church all my life, but religion was—as it was in my mother's childhood home—often reduced to rule keeping. I had no concept of a God who was part of my everyday life. I guess I tried my "performance" out on Him too: being polite at the appropriate moments, attending church regularly, singing in the choir. I suspected that if He was really there, He might be able to see through my pretending. The things I did on Saturday night, you didn't do on Sunday morning in church.

But that night at the concert I heard something I had not heard. Certainly I didn't understand or believe it before.

I was told that I was loved as I was, not as I should be. That my selfishness and foolishness weren't the worst things about me. What was the worst thing that could be said about me? I had stared into the face of perfection and sneered.

What an ugly image. I never remember hating God. I disdained Him through my indifference to Him. Yet He still loved me.

Do you mean I don't have to impress God or perform for His love? Do you mean my life has purpose and value? It seems too good to be true. Yes! *So all those years of trying to prove to my audience that I have the right to live?* They are over now. You have a Savior. His name is Jesus. Say hello; get to know Him. He is pleased to call you His brother.

He comes to me as I am, not as I should be?

Yes.

And He promises He will never leave me or abandon me?

Never!

That was the night my life changed. God sent His Son Jesus to live in the heart of this show-off. He rescued me from the need to save myself through some impossible perfect performance. And He gave me a new reputation to think about.

◊ ◊ ◊

As I began to grow in my new relationship with Jesus, a desire grew within me: the desire to know this God who loved me. I wanted to read a Bible because *He* was in there. A Bible! I wanted to pray because *He* was there. Can you believe it? I even wanted to go to church, and to my surprise He was there too. I discovered profound words that I suspected God wrote just for me. Look at Psalm 139: "O LORD, you have searched me and known me! You know when I sit down" (vv. 1–2 ESV). This is the theme of this song of David's. It is all about what God knows.

And God knows everything about *me*. I'm a little uneasy with that revelation. "You discern my thoughts from afar" (v. 2 ESV). I don't understand my own thoughts, but God does. "Even before a word is on my tongue, behold, O LORD, you know it altogether" (v. 4 ESV). The words I wish I could take back, God knew before they came out.

In those beginning years, what captivated me the most were the pictures David painted in verse 13—"For you formed my inward parts; you knitted me together in my mother's womb"—and in verse 16—"Your eyes saw my unformed substance; in your book were written, every one of them, the days that were formed for me, when as yet there were none of them" (ESV).

Could these verses only be true of David? Is it possible that God could have been there when I was conceived? I'm uncomfortable with that thought. How could God knit me together in my mother's womb? How could He be choosing the chromosomes that would define who I was in the midst of my illegitimate beginning? Could God work through my parents' sin? Could my days be counted by God as though I was planned for? But I wasn't planned for! Or was I? *God, help me understand this!*

It took years—not hours or days, *years*—for me to realize this might not be something I'd ever understand, and that was okay with God. God wasn't asking me to understand it; He was asking me to *believe* it! To believe it not out of a blind faith, but to believe it because of what I knew about Him and in spite of what I knew about me.

That was a crucial first step in discovering a purpose for my life. A reason for my right to live—based not on my parents' poor timing or uncontrolled passions, but on the will of a sovereign God who rules over all and knows all and designs each person.

◊ ◊ ◊

So I no longer needed to be a slave of the need to "perform" for acceptance or worth. But knowing this did not alter the fact that I'd been a slave to the system of performance and reputation building my whole life. That was how I had tried to make life work. These patterns don't go away overnight.

Do I like change? As I've told my students over the years, "The only thing the church hates more than sin is change!" And that's only true because churches are filled with people like me and you. Change is threatening. It challenges our perception that we are in control of life. Which of course we are not. Most of us are barely in control of ourselves, much less our world.

Years after reading Psalm 139 for the first time, after Bible institute and seminary degrees, I was studying the psalm and found myself struggling with the context for those angry words in verses 19–22: "Oh that You would slay the wicked, O God!" (v. 19 ESV).

Wow, where did that come from? As a songwriter, I try to give careful attention to the flow of my lyrics. But the thoughts David had begun developing seem to have just disappeared. He had been talking about how God formed him: "How precious to me are your thoughts, O God! . . . I awake, and I am still with you" (vv. 17–18 ESV). And then out of nowhere: "Do I not hate those who hate you, O LORD?" (v. 21 ESV).

As I read, I was tempted to do what I often do. You probably do the same—skip these verses and go on to the ones you understand. But something kept me there as I tried to figure out why David took this unexpected turn.

He was writing, "I praise you, for I am fearfully and wonderfully made" (v. 14 ESV). And then, "And do I not loathe those who rise up against you? I hate them with complete hatred; I count them my enemies" (vv. 21–22 ESV). Where are all the warm feelings we love about this song?

It would be easy enough to say the Holy Spirit who inspired these words wanted to change the subject now. Why not? He had said all He needs to say about how God knows us and designs us and plans our days. If He wanted David to write about God's enemies, why shouldn't He?

But even more perplexing is what comes next. Immediately after these angry words, we find two verses people have memorized and found comfort in for centuries: "Search me, O God, and know my heart! Try me and know my thoughts! And see if there be any grievous way in me, and lead me in the way everlasting!" (vv. 23–24 ESV). The theme about God searching us is back again. Verse 23 sounds like verse 1 in the present tense. But why here? It feels disjointed after the "loathing" verses. David should have put these first and *then* the angry stuff.

When I was a young Christian, I memorized the first eighteen verses of Psalm 139, ignored the "enemy/anger" verses and memorized the last two verses. I wound up with great verses to meditate on as I was praying with friends.

But can you see yourself in a prayer group with several friends? I can: We take turns praying aloud and quoting from Scripture we've learned, and when it comes my time to pray, I say, "Oh that You would slay the wicked, O God! O men of blood depart from me!" (v. 19 ESV).

More than a few eyebrows are raised. Elbows nudge each other, and eyes that were shut tightly peek open. A moment of silence passes. . . .

"Interesting prayer," says Bobby D. after we all look up. "Did you have a rough day today?" Followed by more awkward silence.

"Is there something you want to tell us, Paul?" asks Joe.

When was the last time you heard these verses memorized? We skip them because we don't know what to do with them. Yet "All Scripture is breathed out by God" (2 Timothy 3:16 ESV). So why did the Holy Spirit inspire David to write these thoughts down in this way?

As I discovered, we need these words more than we can imagine.

◊ ◊ ◊

It was 1994. I had been a university associate professor for eleven years, as well as an academy instructor. Now I had been invited to visit Eastern Europe with a group of fifty Christian professors and teachers from around the United States. I had hoped to visit that part of the world for some time, but when I was told it was Ukraine, I had to find a map and look for the country. I knew almost nothing about it. *Okay, I found it right underneath Russia and above the Black Sea. . . .*

The purpose of our two-week visit was to teach courses on biblical ethics to Ukrainian teachers. Apparently the schools had been dependent on the Communist Party's directives regarding what should be taught and how it should be taught. When perestroika came and Communism was rejected, the teachers weren't sure what to teach or how to control their students, and something akin to anarchy broke out in some schools. So in their desperation, they asked Christian teachers for help.

My colleague and I arrived one day before the other Americans. After settling in at the Russ (roll the "r" and pronounce "oose") Hotel, Richard and I took a cursory look at the beautiful city of Kiev. I survived his snoring that night (bro, you really need to get some help with that), and the following day the rest of the teachers arrived from all over the States. We were strangers to one another; the only thing we had in common was that we were Christian teachers who had been invited to participate in this convocation in Ukraine.

Our first meeting together was an orientation dinner in a beautiful dining room with crystal chandeliers and white lace tablecloths. A buzz of excitement filled the room as we sat down for dinner and began to get to know one another.

The room was divided by columns, as I recall, and arranged mostly in tables for six. My table happened to be at the back right corner of the room. As we enjoyed our dinner of red borscht and varenike (Ukrainian soup and dumplings), I heard something familiar. You know how something you see or hear reminds you of a memory long forgotten, and then in that instant, the memory may as well have been from yesterday? In my case it was a funny laugh, a bit like a machine-gun laugh.

For a second, I remembered that guy at the moving company. I quickly brushed it aside as we often do when the memory is painful. A little later, I heard the sound again—"Eh-eh-eh-eh-eh-eh"—rising above our conversation. I looked up and tried to locate the source of the laugh but realized how crazy that would be and went back to my food. A few minutes later I heard that gun go off again: "Eh-eh-eh-eh-eh-eh."

I pushed myself away from the table, removed my napkin from my lap, stood up, and looked around. I was determined to see where the laugh was coming from so that I could go back to my seat and get on with my dinner.

The sound came from the front of the room, behind one of the columns. As I approached from behind, my pulse began to race. It was impossible! Sitting there with his back to me was *Billy Batson*!

He'd found me! After almost thirty years, he crossed eight time zones and three thousand miles of ocean and he found me in Kiev, Ukraine!

The memories flooded back to me. *Don't the directors of this convocation know who this guy is? This is a group of Christians, for crying out loud—who let him in? Just talk to him for a minute or two and his horrible language should be a clue.*

I tapped him on the shoulder and he turned around. I was shaking as I said, *"Billy Batson!"*

He stood up and looked at me kind of puzzled. He didn't remember me! After all those years, I couldn't forget him and he couldn't remember me! I was insulted again. I looked at him, hardly knowing what to say.

"You and I worked together . . . at United Moving Company, thirty years ago."

"Oh yeah? Well, how are you, brother?"

Brother? Impossible! Then he gave me a bear hug! Never in my life had I imagined getting that close to Billy Batson. Never in my worst nightmares had I *wanted* to get that close to Billy! A Christian?

No!

I didn't want him to become a Christian! I wanted him to get what he deserved. I thought that hell would be a good start as payback for all he'd done to me. *Brother?*

Then I said the only thing I could think to say: "Billy, you really hurt me in those days." He looked at me, and I continued. "Your anger and hate, your intimidation—you made my life miserable!"

And then something amazing happened. Tears formed in Billy's eyes.

"Brother, can you ever forgive me?"

What was I supposed to say?

"Of course I can."

I was lying! I had no intention of forgiving him. And with that lie fresh in my mind I returned to my table. I don't know why, because I had lost my appetite.

I don't remember a thing that was said during the orientation that night. I went to my hotel room and went to bed and tried to sleep. Snoring rumbled across the floor as I stared at the ceiling trying to pray. *God, what's wrong? I can't get Billy out of my mind.*

And God answered me. Not audibly, unfortunately. Not that it would have mattered. I heard Him nevertheless.

"Paul, do you want Me to tell you what your problem is?"

I know what the problem is, Lord. His name is Billy!

"The problem, Paul, is that you think Billy needs forgiveness more than you do."

Well, isn't it obvious, Lord? I mean, look at him! Listen to him!

"Paul, you think Billy needs a Savior more than you do."

I was stopped in my smug, self-righteous tracks. *"You think Billy needs a Savior more than you do."* I couldn't sleep any better than before, but for different reasons.

Now I saw the truth. My heart was a mess. I was arrogant and unwilling to forgive. Most serious of all, I was angry with God that He had saved my enemy. I lay there staring into the night, feeling way too much like Jonah after God had used him to save Nineveh, the archenemy of Israel, from certain destruction. "But it displeased Jonah exceedingly, and he was angry" (Jonah 4:1 ESV).

It's always dangerous, isn't it? When someone else's sins are more obvious to you than your own sins, whether it's your enemy or your spouse. And Psalm 139 finally comes into focus. This song, beautiful in so many ways, may really be a lament. David cries out, *Lord, You know everything there is to know about me—when I sit, when I rise, what I say, what I think, where I am, You designed me.* "If only you would slay the wicked" (v. 19). Can you hear the emphasis on "only"? *If* only *you would slay the wicked." You know it all. Don't you know what the wicked are doing to me? Why don't you stop them?* It's almost as though the rest of the psalm was a setup: *You know this, You know this, You know that . . . but don't You know about my enemies?*

The Holy Spirit who inspired these songs allowed the writers to participate through their feelings and personality and the context of their own lives. This is the context of David's life. He is surrounded by enemies and he wants God to know this and do something.

I am convinced that as the writers of Scripture put down thoughts inspired by the Holy Spirit, sometimes they paused between phrases to reflect on what they had just written. They were sometimes confused, other times moved to tears or praise, and sometimes convicted by what the Spirit told them to write. I imagine that after being inspired to write the words of verses 21 and 22, David paused for a long time— and God spoke to his heart: "I know the struggle you are facing, my son. I'm glad you hate what is evil. And yes, My enemies are your enemies too. But you need to be less the expert in your enemy's sins, and more aware of your own. Less the student of their hearts, and more the student of your own heart."

Maybe David heard the same message I heard: "Your problem is that you think your enemies need forgiveness more than you do. You think they need a Savior more than you need a Savior."

And David's heart is broken over his sin. He responds to the Lord, "Search *me*, O God, and know *my* heart [not my enemies']! Try *me* and know *my* thoughts! And see if there is any grievous way in *me* [not them] and lead *me* in the way everlasting!" (vv. 23–24 ESV).

Do you see? David's confession and his song are for performers like me who too easily find fault in others. We too easily become experts in recognizing everyone else's sins because it takes the pressure off of us. My imperfect performance looks pretty good compared to another's *remarkably* imperfect performance.

I need the Holy Spirit to quiet my anxious, judgmental heart. I want to hear Him remind me that He came to me first, before I ever came to Him. And He continues to come to me and reassure me He still loves me and still saves me.

I didn't stop needing a Savior after I first believed. I still need one, moment by moment, and Slava Bogu (Russian for "praise the Lord"), I have a great Savior in Jesus! This is the gospel—the ongoing, great, good news.

And the Holy Spirit speaks to our hearts. When we are quiet for a moment, we hear Him, and *the kindness of God leads us to repentance* (see Romans 2:4). We needed the gospel. We still do.

◊ ◊ ◊

We will always need the gospel.
Even in the middle of Siberia. . . .

*"Forgotten in
an instant
with one
fraction of
a glimpse of
the One."*

name dropping
in siberia

think of the stories I would tell my friends when I got back home. "There I was teaching and preaching on the frozen tundra, minus-50 degrees outside. I was suffering for Jesus."

So there I was, teaching in an obscure seminary forty-five minutes outside a gray city in the middle of somewhere in Siberia. Believe it or not, I had been looking forward to this trip. It had been snowing in Moscow while I waited for the connecting flight to my "home" for the next week, so I had expected the weather to be even more harsh in Siberia.

But this is a surprisingly vast country. We traveled across three time zones from Moscow to Novosibirsk and—unfortunately for future stories—it was unseasonably warm and raining in Novosibirsk. No snow, no ice, no polar bears in the street. Just mud puddles and gray. Gray coats, gray Stalin-era buildings, and gray weather. Rotten luck! There goes another hook on which to hang my reputation.

Even so, my week was anything but easy. The highlight

was spending a couple of nights with some rock and rollers, barely out of their teens but with honest hearts and a hunger for the truth. During each day I taught a course called the "Grace of Worship" to Russian pastors and students training to be pastors. Sadly, some were the opposite of the rock and rollers, smugly unteachable with less honest hearts. A couple of them talked with each other on cell phones during the class. When I realized what they were doing, I invited them to bring their phones up front and told them, "If you men are the future of the church in Russia, I'm afraid for the church."

Not the way to win friends and influence people, but by that time I didn't care.

Later in the week, as I spoke to one of the more hopeful students, I tried to explain why the students should be willing to listen to me. . . .

It was a mistake.

I should have tried to help him understand why they needed to be willing to learn, but I put the focus on me. "Why don't you listen to me?" My reputation as a Bible teacher was on the line. And having put the focus on myself, I couldn't seem to get out of that rut.

The next thing I knew I was telling this Russian student from Siberia about my teaching credentials, as if it would matter. I told him about my experiences as a conference speaker and about some of the relatively famous people in the United States I have had opportunity to teach—both of them.

"Oh, you don't recognize them? No problem." I reached down a little deeper into my bag of names; I never leave home without them.

I finally found one he knew. This was a tough audience,

this crowd in Siberia—if I couldn't get a standing ovation on the basis of my own reputation, I had no qualms about hitchhiking on someone else's.

In retrospect, I remind myself of a Christian band I heard in concert. If the audience was cold, the band was frigid. So after the band finished another mediocre number, the emcee ran out onto the stage and called to the crowd to give God a hand. If the band couldn't get one, maybe God could!

What did God think about being dragged into the debacle? Surely He has something to say when we use Him, dropping His name because our performance is faltering.

As I defended myself before this seminary student with words on top of more words, I finally let myself be quiet for a moment. I heard the Holy Spirit gently convicting my heart: "It's all about you, Paul, your reputation, your 'right to be listened to.'"

Isn't that often how it is for us when we feel insecure? We just talk and talk.

I went back to my small room in the seminary and sat down on my small bed and asked for forgiveness for my small view of God and my boasting. But as I prayed, admitting my arrogance and unbelief, I began laughing. I couldn't stop.

Father, can You believe it? How deeply does my addiction to reputation run? How desperate is my heart for the approval of others? Here I am, at the end of the earth, surrounded by frozen tundra, thousands of miles from anywhere, trying to impress one man who barely understands English. I'm name dropping in the middle of Siberia!

I couldn't stop laughing. *I'm still tossing them out there, like a drunk tossing down one shot after another. I'm fairly* certain God was laughing, too, and the angels were rejoicing as I turned from my sin.

The next morning, after spending most of my night writing and praying (that was where I began writing this book, in fact), I prepared to fly home and waited for the car to pick me up. My driver overslept, and on the way to the airport his car broke down. We stopped a taxi and then it started snowing—finally—making the roads icy. I was the last person to board the plane and the plane ran out of food before takeoff. Siberian Air. . . . I guess that says it all.

But I was still laughing on my way back to Kiev.

◊ ◊ ◊

The "postmodern" dilemma is a dilemma that spans generations. How do I say I'm wrong and still protect my name? How do I save face while facing my failures?

Our personal pursuit of glory—another way to say "reputation"—makes it difficult to admit the specifics of our personal failure. So I announce I need a Savior, but no one can know what He has saved me from beyond a generic "sin."

And so I cheat people. I don't allow them the opportunity to see the way Jesus has saved me, to see me learning from my struggles. I cheat them of being able to see Jesus at work in the rat's nest my life often becomes. I'm not advocating that we dump all of our garbage on an unsuspecting congregation or dinner party next Sunday. But how about more integrity than simply announcing that you squeeze the toothpaste from the middle of the tube and it drives your wife nuts (which is really more of a confession of your wife's instability than yours, isn't it?).

I think of the young California pastor who stood up and

tearfully announced he had a confession to make. He then asked his wife to come up and stand with him. All of us in the church held our breath waiting for the bombshell.

Had he been unfaithful? Had he cheated on his wife? Maybe he lied about his taxes and now he had been found out?

Here came the confession. Drum roll, please. . . .

"I haven't spent enough time with my wife!" And everyone let out a huge sigh of relief.

Everyone but me. I was mad.

Now, you would think I'd be glad it wasn't worse, and it is important to spend time with your wife, but this felt like a setup. The pastor had gone on and on, making it sound as if this was going be a dark secret finally coming to light. He manipulated us into thinking that this was as bad as life got for him. If not spending time with his wife was the worst thing he had done, who could identify with him?

But I had inside information. This same pastor had shared with me about his personal ongoing battle with lust. A battle most of his elders probably ached over. And yet as far as his congregation was concerned, his example of an emotional heart-wrenching confession had to do with time management.

He cheated his people, and I would bet others saw through this "hollow" confession too.

Was it all for the sake of protecting *image*? After all "image is everything," isn't it?

◊ ◊ ◊

In the churches of Ukraine, where Gail and I live and work, it's rare if not impossible to hear repentance practiced or modeled from the pulpit.

Preached, yes. Leaders even place microphones in front of the congregation and invite people to walk down and announce to the church the struggles of their heart, and I've often wept with those sincere people. But seldom will you hear the leaders admit to personal failure beyond saying, "I'm weak too. I struggle like you do."

They are trying to save face. What an odd expression. Whose face needs saving and from what? Why do they do this anyway?

One reason is cultural.

During the seventy years of Communism in Ukraine, nobody in any sphere of life wanted to take responsibility for poorly made decisions. The consequences were too severe. You could lose your job, your flat, your freedom, even your life. But certainly you lost your good reputation. As a result, it was difficult to find anyone in authority who would take responsibility for *any* decision, just in case it turned out to be a wrong one. This is why the red tape (excuse the pun) here is unbelievable today.

This reluctance to make a poor decision for the sake of reputation carried over into the Ukrainian church. For instance, pastors may be reluctant to attend seminary because they don't want to be seen as one *needing* to learn something, for fear of losing the respect of fellow pastors. How do pastors admit to hurting a brother or sister without losing face? How do Christian leaders admit struggles with any specific sin, such as gossip or jealousy, much less the more "indictable" ones like rage or lust?

Leaders in and beyond Ukraine are afraid to confess their own weakness because they fear the consequences are too severe. *I'll lose my credibility as a godly leader, or worse, I'll lose my power.* Even those who don't believe in

God can see through that hypocrisy. That's one reason we leaders often have so little credibility in the world. Why does this happen? If you work in ministry, you probably don't get paid too much and you can't drive the best cars. Often you are resentful that you feel the need to play this charade of false humility. The only thing you still have is your reputation. Then God has the nerve to ask you to sacrifice that as well and admit your weakness for the sake of His glory. It's too much to ask.

Whether we are in formal leadership roles or not, underneath any cultural reasons for our self-protection are pride and unbelief. We misunderstand something. We think others will be drawn to Christ by our changed life, but it's our *changing* life that connects our realities with their realities. That's what interests them: the process, the in-between.

But maybe there is more to this than simply protecting reputation. Maybe we are not so sure that God is saving and changing us. Maybe we're not sure the reputation we are guarding is worth protecting. And if others found out about *that*, where would we be?

◊ ◊ ◊

Listen to the opening line of *The Patriot*, spoken by Mel Gibson's character: "I have long feared that my sins would return to me, and the cost is more than I can bear."

I too have lived with that fear. The fear that my past sins were so ingrained in me I would never be free from them.

At the end of Romans 8 is a great promise I memorized as a young believer: "For I am convinced that neither death nor life, neither angels nor demons, neither the present nor the future, nor any powers, neither height nor depth," [and just in case Paul forgot something . . .] *"nor anything else in all creation,* will be able to separate us from the love of God that is in Christ Jesus our Lord" (vv. 38–39). What great comfort in this promise from God.

But recently I saw something I had missed before. Did you see it? Paul writes, "neither the present nor the future." What is missing?

The past!

Paul forgot to cover that.

Or maybe not.

God regards the past as past. It's gone. "[I] will remember their sins no more" (Jeremiah 31:34). God doesn't tell us the past won't separate us from His love because the past is already dead! It's not a factor.

The only one who wants to keep my awful past alive and in my face is Satan.

And the voices come back, don't they?

The accuser does what accusers always do: dredge up the past, put new clothes on it, call it the present and future, beat you to death with it, and then condemn you to hell.

Paul writes to the church in Philippi, "But one thing I do . . ." (Philippians 3:13). This verse is not vague. One thing— not many things that I do.

What is that one thing you do, Paul?

"Forgetting what is behind and straining toward what is ahead . . ." (v. 13). The past is past.

"I have long feared that my sins would return to me, and the cost is more than I can bear." If I bear my own sins, I can guarantee they will come back, and with a vengeance. But doesn't the gospel teach us that only Jesus can bear our sins, and He does?

I have been afraid that my sins were too much even for

Jesus to deal with. I have minimized the cross and made
little of the blood of Christ. I have believed the wrong voices.
Forgive me, Jesus.
And then we are afraid forgiveness won't take. We don't
want to step out of the phone booth like Superman until the
suit is all there. Understandable, right? What is Superman if
he forgets his cape or has his S on backward? How embarrassing could that be?

So we hide in our rooms trying to get that S twisted
around the right way, but people don't care. They are struggling with thoughts about adultery and bulimia and greed
and they want someone who is honest about his or her
struggle to come alongside in the middle of the process.

But how do I allow others to see myself in this process
of changing?

◊ ◊ ◊

I decided to ask my wife a dangerous question. I got the
idea from Jack Miller. My advice to you: don't ask it if you
don't want to know the truth.

I asked my wife: "Gail, if you could change one thing
about me, what would it be?" I think I added, "Only one,"
since my heart wasn't ready for more.

You would like to think she'd need some time to think
about it, right? Don't count on it. Gail needed about thirty
seconds. No, less than that.

"If I could change one thing about you, Paul, it would
be this: that you would believe how much God loves you."

Wow! She knows me! At first I was relieved that she
chose that sin when she could have picked some sins I
considered more embarrassing and more painful, but she
went much deeper than I expected. And the soliloquy of

"Voices" speaks once again:

> *When will I know it's You?*
> *When will I know You are here?*
> *In the dull and distance of uncertainty,*
> *when will I know You still love me,*
> *and when is that enough . . . ?*

In Galatians Paul cuts through all the law-keeping we hide behind and tells us how to connect faith with the love of God. Paul writes in Galatians 5:6, "The only thing that counts . . ." (Now if the apostle Paul says the "only" thing that counts, don't you want to know what it is? "Only" eliminates a lot of other things, doesn't it?) "The only thing that counts is faith expressing itself through love."

God's love has come to performers like you and me who could never dance perfectly enough to deserve heaven's applause and could not fall badly enough to forfeit it. This love is infinitely beyond our personal show. The spotlight never was on us—it has always been, and always will be, on Him! When I believe this, I am able to enjoy the truth and extend the same kind of love to those people I work, study, and play with. Gail is right. I need to let go of trying to be good enough for such love and start believing it.

In the first chapter of Galatians, we hear this emotional outburst from Paul to the church: "I am *astonished* that you are so quickly deserting . . ." Note what follows. It isn't the doctrine about grace Paul mentions; he will deal with that, too, but not first: ". . . you are so quickly deserting the one who called you" (v. 6).

The church in Galatia is confused about law and grace because their relationship with God is broken. It is God they are deserting, it is God they have stopped loving—and they have become unable to accept or extend His love because of this breakdown of relationship.

It isn't our dutiful work as a husband or wife, mother or father, daughter or friend that counts. It isn't our titles: pastor, bishop, professor, teacher, pope, or missionary. *"The only thing that counts is faith expressing itself through love."*

If I struggle to love well, scolding won't help me love better. What renders me such a poor lover of Jesus and others? It is the very thing my wife saw. I struggle to believe that God loves me. When I don't believe, I don't love.

My turning from sin needs to begin here. *Forgive me, Father, for not believing You love me.*

This isn't a formula. This is not simply a matter of following some steps in order to guarantee loving well.

It's a process. And it's something others need to see.

◊ ◊ ◊

They say confession is good for the soul. Some might add, "But it's bad for the reputation."

From the time I was a boy I struggled with pornography. I remember having a stash of magazines hidden under the mattress and behind the drawers in my room. One night I had a nightmare related to some of the images I had seen earlier that night.

I awoke so scared and so disgusted that I got up. I gathered my supply of magazines, quietly walked downstairs, and put them in a pile by the trashcan, an appropriate place for them. I intended to throw them out early the next morning, before they were discovered by anyone else.

Shortly after I went back to sleep, my door opened.

It was my mother.

This was my second nightmare of the night but this time I was wide awake.

You guessed it.

She heard me get up and after I went back to sleep she decided to see what I had been doing.

She went down to the basement and found my pile. I don't even want to remember the look on her face. She immediately must have thought that her own sins had come back to haunt her. *I knew this was inevitable for the son of my own shame.*

Needless to say, I was in sooo much trouble.

But when she confronted me about it, I told her the truth. "I hate those magazines and I'm getting rid of them, even without you or anyone else knowing about them or telling me to."

It was one of those special times when she recognized that even then God was working on my heart. No additional discipline followed. No more scolding. She saw God taking care of her son in His own way.

But for much of my life, whenever I stopped trusting God, this habitual sin came back to trap me.

◊ ◊ ◊

Trapped

Ask the miner underground, "How do you feel?"
Trapped by earth and rock, the tunnel home is
  sealed!
From the darkness the reply—a muffled, hopeless
  shout,
"The walls around caved in on me and there is no
  way out."

Ask the diver in the sea, "How do you feel?"
Her feet are hopelessly trapped in weeds of steel.
From the depths—could she reply—would come a
*   frantic shout,*
"It seems the more I struggle here, the more my
*   strength gives out."*

Ask the prisoner of desire,
ruled by passion's fire,
and from a mind that's torn in two
his heart can barely shout,
"God I hate the trap I'm in, I hope no one finds out."

Ask the One who made us, "How do You feel?"
The Holy One who forgives can also heal.
From a heart that breaks with love, He's crying out,
"The stone's been rolled away, the Son's been raised
no need to doubt.
Don't you know? Your Father hears His children
*   shout!"*

◊ ◊ ◊

In more recent years, God has given me such grace and power in this area. Where does that power come from? Ironically, from believing in the love of God. *"The kindness of God. . . ."* That particular stronghold has been broken and I am enjoying a peace and freedom I never thought would be possible. I am watching God's promises connect with my daily choices. Am I perfect? No. But the past is past. My old nature is still active, but it is no longer my master.

Paul writes in Romans, "And we know that in all things God works for the good of those who love him, who have been called according to his purpose" (8:28). He goes on to identify that purpose: "For those God foreknew he also predestined to be conformed to the likeness of his Son" (8:29).

And that's it. That's the purpose He called us to in the previous verse: *to be made in the image of His Son, Jesus,* to be known by His name and not my own.

"How does God do this?" you ask.

Do you really want to know?

◊ ◊ ◊

You might want to bring a flashlight with you. It's surprising how dark it can get in here. . . .

painting
in the dark

*"No time or
space or words
could tame the
One powerful to
create yet wise to
transcend those
limitations."*

It took some time to get the room exactly the way it needed to be. The ceilings were high with large windows at the top. These would have to be covered completely with black paper. The door would be opened by latecomers. There had to be a way to minimize the shock of light blasting into the room when that happened.

A black curtain was suspended on a six-foot square frame and was hung immediately in front of the door. Everyone would enter through this curtain. *Good, this will heighten their expectations, make them curious, even uncomfortable.* A sign posted outside warned late arrivers to enter carefully and quietly. The chairs were set in rows as usual, with an aisle down the middle.

I sat nervously in front, making small talk with friends as people quickly filled the room. I wasn't nervous because of fearfulness but from an excitement that others sensed as well—the anticipation of something special. And this was going to be special by most definitions.

It was time for my Bible class to begin. I stood up, faced the students, and said, "When we first believed in Jesus, we blew dust off a Bible and read: 'If anyone is in Christ, he is a new creation' [2 Corinthians 5:17]. That was great! That was what we needed. The old person was a mess."

I continued, "The old has gone, the new has come! We began to experience the truth of these verses. We imagined —or at least hoped—that everything would change overnight. That chocolate cake would no longer be tempting, that we would stop being so impatient, and that we would no longer look down on all the little people around us."

The class laughed.

"'You are my lamp, O Lord,' David writes in 2 Samuel 22:29. 'The Lord turns my darkness into light.' Peter promises us that God has 'called you out of darkness into his wonderful light' [1 Peter 2:9]. We wanted change to be as dramatic as dark to light. We wanted a new world that would be as different from the old as night from day."

I took one last long look at my notes.

Suddenly the room became black as the blackest night, not even a hint of light! *Good, right on cue. And that black paper over those windows is shutting out all light from the outside hallway. Perfect!* A curious buzz passed across the rows.

"Don't panic." I was glad the darkness hid my smile—I suppose I hoped for a little panic. "Yes, the electric bills have been paid. And no, this is not an accidental power outage." The room became relatively quiet.

"Today we'll try to understand and feel what Jesus really meant when He prayed to the Father about you and me."

Which prayer was that?

Jesus was sitting in the Upper Room in Jerusalem with

His disciples. He had washed their feet, eaten with them, and had the first Communion with them. Now Jesus looks around the table at these men He has loved and taught for three years. John, the disciple who is remembering this unforgettable night, was reclining next to Him.

Jesus begins to pray for them out loud and laughter and arguments stop as the disciples recognize what Jesus is doing. One disciple nudges another one with "Shh" and another conversation stops in mid-sentence. They listen to Jesus pray, "My prayer is not that you [our Father] take them [you and me] out of the world . . ." (John 17:15).

If we could have been in that room, don't you know we would have seen more than a few eyebrows raised and heard some protests made? We might have joined in: "But Jesus, why not? If heaven is perfect, just ask the Father to take us there immediately!"

Jesus goes on to say what He is asking for: ". . . but that you protect them from the evil one" (v. 15).

What just happened?

Judas has been filled with Satan and has left the room to go betray Jesus to the high priest. The disciples don't know why Judas left, but Jesus knows and is painfully aware that He will be going to the cross in only a few hours—because of Satan and his evil work. Jesus knows that to leave us in the world was to leave us in a place where Satan could attack us, so He asks the Father to protect us.

We need protection in this world. It's a dangerous place; it's a dark and cursed place. God left me here and I'd like to know why. What does it mean to be "in the world, but not of it"?

Back in our own classroom, we could feel it. The dark. The chill that seems to creep into a room when the light has been frightened off. The darkness even has a certain smell. Or maybe it's that our other senses kick in when the sense of sight is taken away. *I did take a shower . . . didn't I?*

I glanced around the blackness. This was better than I had hoped for!

"Before we knew Jesus, we lived in darkness. This darkness surrounding us today is a picture of the world of the lost. All of us are reluctant to remember it, but we do remember something about how blind we were then. 'How could we have missed the truth for so long?' we ask. But a more insightful question might be, 'How were we ever able to find the truth in such blackness?'

"You see, some of us actually imagine that we were better than we were. Kinder than most people, more forgiving, more appreciative. It's a little bit like being around an old guy telling stories of his youth. He smiles as he tells us he was the best football player in his neighborhood. Who's still around to tell us he was kind of clumsy? He winks as he reminds us he was the fastest kid in school.

"It would be easy to hear my own sons laughing right now and saying, 'That's you, Dad!' Our memory has a way of polishing up the past. As a friend of mine says, while it's true that we start to lose our memory as we get older, the good news is that we get to meet a lot of new people. Sometimes one of the new people you meet is you!"

I continued from the front of the class to talk about how we forget our heart's true condition before we knew Jesus. We vaguely recall that while some people were blind, we were only a little shortsighted.

This loss of memory on our part explains why we relate so poorly to those outside the faith today and fail so miserably in our attempts at connecting with them. In our most honest moments we might admit we prefer to avoid them. We find ourselves impatient. *Why are they so slow to get it? Why can't they just believe like I do!*

I forget where I came from and can't identify with those still there. I insist that they act like people of the light. But they can't; they don't have the power. Neither did I. So why do I think I have the right to look down on them?

Those who don't believe are just as smart as believers. Some are smarter. They are just as talented as believers. Many are more talented. They love their children and so do we. Some are happy in their marriages and some of us are too. How are they different from us? We are not better than they are because God had mercy on us. They're lost, like we were. But it's so easy to forget that.

What is it that marks us as different from people who do not yet believe or who may never believe? Is it our bumper stickers, nervous smiles, or quick answers to long questions? In Exodus 33, Moses is pleading with God not to abandon Israel. He says, "What else will distinguish me and your people from all the other people on the face of the earth [if your Presence does not go with us]?" (v. 16).

The real difference is the presence of God with us. Immanuel in us. Not our "performance," but the way we allow God in us to love others through us. But I forget so quickly and love so poorly.

Our loss of memory also helps explain why we are so surprised by our personal failures and so discouraged and angry because of life's twists and turns. We have unrealistic expectations about ourselves and life now. We feel shame over what still tempts us and hopelessness over the ongoing consequences of past sins.

By the way, is it a sin to be tempted? No? But I find myself often confessing my temptations: *Lord, please forgive me for being so easily tempted to worry.*

If you are tempted to covet someone's new Mercedes, does this make you a coveter? If you are tempted to commit adultery, does this make you an adulterer? Do your temptations define you? If so, we are all in such trouble!

Jesus was tempted as we are, yet was without sin. So, being tempted only means we are human. But in the dark, that is easy to forget. We live with a lot of unnecessary guilt because of it. Once we were all equally prisoners of the dark, The People of the Dark. And there is no hiding our deep disappointment and irritation that we still share the same space.

◊ ◊ ◊

I moved carefully to the center of our black room. I was guessing where I was going, of course.

"Oh, by the way, there was a mistake made when you first entered the room and sat down. All of you on the right side of my voice were supposed to be sitting on the other side of the room. And those of you on the left side were supposed to be sitting on the right side. I need to ask you to stand now and find your correct seats on the opposite side of the room."

What noise erupted from these normally well-mannered businessmen, doctors, lawyers, and musicians! "Watch out" was heard from all sides (as if anyone could see). The room had become instant chaos! Grown men and women began giggling like schoolchildren.

"Shhh. Is it easy to move in the dark?" I asked helpfully.

"No. Ow! That's my foot you're standing on."

There was nervous laughter, louder than the joke

deserved, because that's what nervous people do in the dark. They laugh at nothing at all.

"Did you move quickly or slowly?"

"Slowly."

"Is change welcomed in the dark?"

A voice stuck somewhere in the middle of a row responded, "No!"

"Are you more generous or more selfish in the dark?"

"Selfish," as one woman poked an elbow into the man next to her, assuming this was the same husband she began the class with.

"Why?"

"You have to guard what you have. Someone might steal it and no one could see who did it."

Someone else added, "And if you give everything away where will you go to replace it? No, we are definitely more selfish."

"Let's talk about values."

I then felt around the table for a painting I'd placed there face down earlier. Holding it up I asked, "What do you think of this painting?"

"What painting?"

I ignored the question.

"Do you like the artist's use of reds and greens? Where do you think the focal point is? . . . Hard to tell in the dark, isn't it? And yet, people painting in the dark have turned out masterpieces.

"There are others living in the dark who hang urinals on the walls of art galleries and call it art. How do you recognize good art from bad in the dark, good music from bad?

"How about the arguments put forth about the right to abort a baby in his or her mother's womb? If someone doesn't know the value of a mother in the dark, how can he know the value of life inside the mother in the dark? Living in the dark is no excuse for sin, but it is an explanation."

I put the painting down.

"So how do we know basic truths and values in the dark—truths about art and life, its value and purpose? We can know for the same reason we can meditate on the beauty of a sunset and be hypnotized by a spring shower.

"Theologians call this *common grace*. Not common in the sense of ordinary with little worth but common in the sense that it is available to all of us. This is God's design of humankind, made in His image: we can distinguish beautiful from ugly. Even selfish people can recognize extraordinary as well as ordinary design. There is so much grandeur and compassion and generosity in the dark. And we are all able to feel our hearts stir with a soaring melody and feel love and love being loved. Common grace doesn't seem so common if we really think about it."

I asked the class, "A moment ago when you were moving in the dark, and someone, you don't know who, accidentally brushed up against your arm, were you indifferent to it or startled by it?"

"Startled."

"Did you pull back instinctively?"

Someone emboldened by the darkness answers, "I wasn't sure whether to feel good or bad about a stranger's touch. I'm not sure what to feel guilty about in the dark."

"Maybe it's easier to ignore or rationalize what I do. I can blame it on the dark."

"We may feel guilty about everything or nothing in the dark."

"Yes! Welcome to what C. S. Lewis called *Shadowland*.

This is where we lived before we knew Christ. I'm glad I don't live there anymore. Aren't you?"

I paused. A little silence goes a long way in the dark.

"But what if the Father heard the prayer of His Son? Doesn't the Father always hear His Son's prayers? What if the Father took seriously the request of Jesus? Why wouldn't He?

"'My prayer is not that you take them out of the world . . .' Is it possible that we have had the wrong expectations? We thought that when we became Christians all of the lights would be turned on for us, no more stumbling in the dark. We hoped that all questions would be answered, all doubts would be put away, and all fears would scurry back to the past where they came from.

"Listen to the apostle Paul as he writes to the believers in the city of Colossae: 'He [God] has delivered us from the domain of darkness and transferred us to the kingdom of his beloved Son' [Colossians 1:13 ESV]. There is the proof we wanted, right there. Once we give our hearts to Christ we no longer live in the dark, right?

"But before someone goes too far with that argument, consider this. The word *domain* used in this passage actually means "authority," or as some translations read, "dominion." We who have trusted in Jesus have been rescued from Satan's dominion—his authority.

"As Martin Luther wrote in the hymn 'A Mighty Fortress Is Our God': 'The Prince of Darkness grim, we tremble not for him; His rage we can endure.' Satan rules with delegated authority over those who have not believed in Jesus. I am not under Satan's control anymore, yet I still live in a dark place.

"Why else would Jesus call us 'the light of the world'

[Matthew 5:14]? Why else would God promise that His Word is a lamp to our feet and a light to our path in Psalm 119 if we didn't still need a light? If we were no longer living in a dark world, these figures of speech would be unnecessary.

"Why would John write in his first letter, 'If we walk in the light, as he is in the light' [1 John 1:7] unless we need to choose whether to walk in light or darkness? *If* implies maybe we will and maybe we won't.

"We expected it to be different and the darkness has caught us off guard. But this may explain a lot to us. Why do I sometimes stumble so easily? Why does life often look a great deal like it did before I became a Christian? And, Lord, why am I so angry with You sometimes? I expected You to fix everything for me, but You didn't. You want me to find You and You want me to do Your will, but it's not so easy to find You or Your will in pitch darkness.

"Yes, we are the light of the world! Yes, we have His Word as a light, and yes we forget to trust God and His light.

"Solomon tells us in Ecclesiastes 11, 'Light is sweet, and it pleases the eyes to see the sun. However many years a man may live, let him enjoy them all. But let him remember the days of darkness, for they will be many' [vv. 7–8]. Notice how he changes tenses here; he connects the past, the present, and the future.

"What is Solomon's advice? 'Give up, it's just going to get worse anyway'? No, but the wisest man who lived understood that darkness is the world in which we live. He counsels us not to forget it, but we still forget.

"Sometimes I 'punish' God for not turning on all the lights right now, not later, and I pout. I withdraw from Him, refusing to pray or read His Word, or go to church, thinking

I can force Him to do what He otherwise might not do. I hope God will say, 'All right, Paul, I see how my decision has hurt your feelings and I'm sorry. I'll try to take better care of you, with less pain, more backrubs, fewer embarrassing moments or days or . . .'

"Here then is our big surprise in the darkness: we aren't in heaven yet! And life is tough, and we still stub our toes in the dark, and worse."

I moved to the podium where I had concealed a flashlight. I suddenly turned it on, only for a second or two. Of course, it would be cruel to shine that harsh light in some poor unsuspecting person's face. . . . Eyes blinked with shock and then shut immediately.

"Excuse me. I thought you would welcome the light after so much time spent in the dark." (Sarcasm is easily spotted even in the dark.) I turned off the light and moved toward someone else.

"It is easier than we thought to become accustomed to the dark. Now, we who are children of the light are actually a bit uncomfortable with the light."

I interrupted someone else's darkness with a shot from my flashlight. Her eyes blinked back the intruder and retreated under sealed eyelids. Again I apologized, though most were suspecting my apology to be less than sincere.

"Now, if the light bothers you, imagine what it must feel like to those who are yet prisoners of the Prince of Darkness.

"Here is a useful principle to remember: *a little light goes a long way in the dark!*

"Back off on preaching to your lost relatives every time you get together. Listen at least as much as you talk. Listening allows people time to get used to the light. Listening encourages people not to be so afraid of the light.

"But Jesus captures another reality in John 3:19–20: 'And this is the judgment: the light has come into the world, and people loved the darkness rather than the light because their deeds were evil. For everyone who does wicked things hates the light and does not come to the light, lest his deeds should be exposed'" (ESV).

I aimed my voice toward someone sitting by the door. "Please turn the lights on in the room now." Eyes blinked shut everywhere as light flooded into the room and protests erupted again from normally agreeable folks.

"A little light goes a long way in the dark. Why would I try to force decisions by drowning my friends in guilt, and then defend myself by saying, 'I just don't want to see them go to hell'?

"It isn't my job to save. That's the work of the Holy Spirit. I can relax and love them as they are, not withholding my love until they believe. But it's easier to say than to do. I'm still stuck here painting in the dark, wondering how this is going to help me look like Jesus.

"So here are two big surprises we are learning in the dark. First, we aren't in heaven yet. We who love Jesus have been left in this world, and we didn't expect it to be so dark. But it was God's plan for us, because we don't trust God unless we have to. It's the way we are and God knows this.

"Second, we need protection from the evil one because we are still living where he roams as a roaring lion, seeking those whom he may devour" [see 1 Peter 5:8].

I left the lights on for the remainder of that class. That time spent in the dark was eye opening for many of us. But life doesn't have light switches that we can turn on and off at will. We collide with people in the dark, and when we do, we often hurt each other.

◊ ◊ ◊

One time my dad was apologizing to someone for something I'd done. Maybe I was fifteen or sixteen years old. "Paul has always had trouble with the truth," he said as he smiled a kind of smug smile that really hurt. It didn't feel like love, and it took me a while to forgive him for that. We can destroy each other with careless and arrogant words.

Whose face do you see when you are asked who you need to forgive? Who has hurt you?

If I asked you to name who you struggle to get along with, maybe to the point of regarding him or her as an enemy, whose name is whispered in your ear? Is it an ex-husband or a deceptive manager?

Would I have said Billy Batson? Would somebody else say Paul Thorson?

The apostle Paul writes about right relationships in Ephesians 5 and 6. His words about "how to do relationships" are not suggestions; they are directives from our sovereign God and King.

Yet we often forget how to care for each other in this dark place. We husbands regard our wives as the enemy, and they return the "look." We think this is just the way life is. You are my friend, yet I justify my unwillingness to trust you. And you return the favor.

We forget the prayer of Jesus in John 17. We forget that we have an enemy who tries to sucker punch us in this blackness and in the confusion trick us into thinking someone else is to blame. And we lash out at the closest person to us simply because we can see him.

When I was young, I used to wrestle. I reached my peak in wrestling when I was in seventh grade—well, maybe later. One thing about wrestling is never in doubt: you never have to wonder who your adversary is. There is no one on that mat but you and your opponent.

I will never forget the first time I wrestled a blind opponent. The referee took him by the hand and led him to the center of the mat, facing me. Then the referee placed my hand in contact with the other wrestler's hand, stepped back and blew his whistle, and the match began. Every time we lost physical contact with each other the whistle would blow, contact would be reestablished, and the match would continue. We each knew who the adversary was.

God has deliberately selected the word *wrestling* to describe our struggle with the "spiritual forces of evil" in Ephesians 6:12. He wants us to be crystal clear about who our enemy is.

When I hear the voices accusing me, or accusing someone else in my thoughts, and I can't see who it is in the darkness, I need to remember who is really on the mat with me. It isn't my roommate or coworker or wife. I need to remember it is Satan I face. My enemy is the same one who tempted Adam and Eve in the garden—and Jesus in another garden.

◊ ◊ ◊

When we first came to Ukraine in 1994, I was a guest professor of composition at the Kiev State Conservatory. I was not asked to preach to my music students; I was asked to teach composition courses on "American song-style." My wife, an artist, was a student of one of Ukraine's great watercolor artists, Yuri Ivanovich Himich. Neither of us spoke any Russian and we were helpless without our interpreters. We came into a culture that was rich in the arts and we determined to let the people of Ukraine teach us.

The result was the beginning of some wonderful friendships with artists and musicians, most of whom were not believers. The friendships continue, and the light is being seen. Many of the lost are still the lost, but they know we love them and they let us speak into their lives. We let them speak into our lives too. But it is dark here. We feel it daily and it wears us out and we wish we had some measure of control over life here—but control is hard to find in the dark.

I walk in the light as I put my trust in God. When I stop trusting in Jesus, I lose the benefit of His light. And this leads us to our third surprise.

There is another darkness that all of us must deal with. This one is more personal to each of us, more insulting to our reputation than any of us care to admit.

When I came to Christ, I was given a new nature, and this new nature is the truest thing about me. This is who I am now. But my old nature is still with me. It no longer is my master, but it still influences me. And if I understand Ephesians 4:22, "Put off your old self, which is being corrupted by its deceitful desires," the sense of "being corrupted" implies that the corruption is continuing.

What else can that mean except that my flesh is getting worse and worse? According to A. Skevington Wood, "The old self is subject to an internal process of disintegration. The present tense 'is being corrupted' reveals that it is continuous. Moral degeneration has set in."[1] This explains why a man who has been a Christian leader and pastor for years and seemingly happily married can suddenly run off with his church secretary. How can a godly man do something so terrible?

None of us can afford to "coast" in our spiritual life. Our old nature is not only still there, it is even more evil than before we knew Jesus—it is getting more and more corrupt.

You and I know how shocked we are sometimes by the thoughts we have: "How could I even imagine such a thing?" Our flesh is capable of not only imagining but doing anything.

That's why the flesh isn't something to fix, but something to die to. "Therefore do not let sin reign in your mortal body so that you obey its evil desires" (Romans 6:12). The evil desires still lurk in the shadows. Paul says in Galatians 5:16, "Walk by the Spirit, and you will not gratify the desires of the flesh" (ESV).

Notice, Paul does not say "Walk by the Spirit and you will not have desires of the flesh." Why? Because we do have evil desires in the flesh. Our responsibility is to refuse to gratify these desires. We need the Holy Spirit working this truth into our hearts and actions.

We see how deceptive our enemy is. He feeds us these evil desires, then accuses us of having them, and then accuses God in our thoughts: *Why did God let me have these awful thoughts?* And so we need more truth, more of the gospel. More light on the way to dying to self and becoming like Jesus.

If I listen carefully I can hear Jesus continuing to pray for me here in a dark place. So can you: "Father . . . my prayer is not that You take them out of the world, but that You protect them from the evil one."

◊ ◊ ◊

All children go through a phase when their
favorite response to everything is, "It's not fair!"
Some of us never outgrow that phase. . . .

the cliffs
of fairness

*"All attempts
to paint and
sculpt, to
compose His
likeness, lie
incomplete,
inspired dust."*

t he student in the front row of the class could stand it no longer and raised her hand. Not waiting for me to recognize her, she blurted out, "It is so unfair!"

I had been talking about God's right to call people to Himself and had quoted Jesus in John 6:44, "No man can come to me unless the Father who sent me draws him."

She went on, "What about people who've never heard of Jesus? They don't have a chance. What about them?" She became more animated as her words tumbled out. "It's like all humankind is standing on the highest cliff and we all fall off. Waiting at the bottom of the cliff is *hell*. Then God reaches out His hand and randomly catches one person over here and then another one over there, as others sail on by into hell. How fair is that?"

This particular student had perfect marks in school; she was very bright and right now very agitated.

"What a profound question!"

Too often students seem afraid to think, and it's important to help them understand that we have permission to ask God the hardest questions. I became excited about the thoughts that were pouring into my mind as I considered her words.

I said that her analogy was a great start but suggested we change it a little to see if we could find out what "fair" really is regarding our relationship to God.

"So, all of humankind is gathered on a cliff. But standing there, we suddenly feel someone else is present. Like the feeling we have when walking at night and we sense that there is someone closing in behind us. A foreboding type of feeling. Our heart is pounding, our pulse racing, we don't know who or what is there and we are afraid to look over our shoulder and see. As we turn around to see who it is we let out a collective scream. 'Aiiii! Quick, jump! It's a *holy* God!' We don't fall; we *jump* off the cliff together, to escape God.

"You see, I don't want to go to hell, but in that moment, staring into those holy eyes, I'd rather be anywhere else. Heaven only feels like heaven to those who are at peace with the King of heaven. In Romans 5, we read that those who are justified by faith have peace with God (see v. 1).

"But this is unthinkable for enemies of God. And Paul calls those who don't know Jesus 'enemies' just a few verses later in this same chapter in Romans (v. 9). At the time God found us, we were not longing for peace with God; we wanted victory over God, or at least protection from the wrath of God. We weren't looking for Him; we were hiding from Him."

I looked around the room and saw that the students were with me—we had all jumped. (As I reflect back, I wish I'd improvised on a scene from *Dead Poets Society* and had all the students stand on their chairs and jump off at the count of three.)

"This is where your analogy becomes so interesting," I said. "All of humankind has jumped off the cliff and we are falling into hell. And yes, God reaches His hand down to catch some people. Suddenly the hand catches a woman falling near me. I instinctively curl up, hoping He won't notice me. And as the woman vanishes, I turn to a guy near me and wipe my forehead, 'Whew, that was close. For a second there I thought He was after me!' He nods his head in agreement, never taking his eyes off that spot where the woman had been moments before.

"Once again the hand appears; the man I was talking to is gone. Oh, no! Again I feel real terror. 'The poor guy . . .' No sooner do the words escape my lips then the hand appears again. But this time I feel a sudden change come over me and I realize two things at once: *The hand is coming for me; there is no escape.* And, *My heart is willing; now I want Him to catch me.* And He does! And it is wonderful, not terrifying, and it is perfect, not terrible."

Our arguments for "fairness" presuppose that we are wiser than God. We think that we deserve a chance to know God. But even the idea that we first wanted to know Him is a deception. And when we realize this, we realize the foolishness of believing we have a reputation worth protecting in the first place.

◊ ◊ ◊

We have missed the point in our arguments about whether it is fair of God to choose some people for Himself but not choose others. We assume that everyone wants to be chosen and those who are not feel somehow cheated.

When did a soldier in battle ever want to be captured by his enemy? Or feel cheated if he escaped capture? When did a true sportsman ever long to be conquered by his fiercest opponent? Why do we think it's any different in the battle between a sinful world and a holy God?

The real question is this: Why does God want to love such enemies as you and me? Why is it that God "so loved the world that he gave his one and only Son"(John 3:16)? Why would He bother to reach His hand down and catch even one of us? If He can create everything with a single word, why not wipe the slate clean and start over with people who will trust and not rebel? What would that take—two words? Probably just the thought would be enough.

Not only are we not worthy, we don't even want to be saved for God. We only want to be saved *from* God. Jesus says that in hell "there will be weeping and gnashing of teeth" (Matthew 8:12). The weeping is easy to understand— it will be unending torment, the "unquenchable fire" (see Matthew 3:12). Of course people will cry there; that's why it's called hell. But maybe those tears you see aren't tears of a repentance that has come too late. Perhaps those are not the tears of reluctant sinners and postmodern innocents whose only mistake was their reticence to make a commitment. Maybe those are angry tears. That is what "gnashing of teeth" suggests.

Can you picture some villain in handcuffs in a B movie grinding his teeth together and snarling at the hero, "I'll get you, if it takes me the rest of my life," as they haul him off to jail? That is "gnashing of teeth." That is the intense anger of someone who bitterly hates God. He isn't filled with thoughts of regret for his sin. He is filled with thoughts of revenge. If he could get his hands on God, he'd strangle the life out of Him!

At the root of any true discussion of fairness must be the question, "How good is God?" Followed by, "How bad is humankind?" We in the church have not done well on the test. We've missed the answer to both questions and then preached sermons, written books, and recorded songs built on our wrong answers.

God's capacity for goodness infinitely exceeds my definitions of fairness. And my capacity for evil is deeper than my willingness or ability to fathom.

My complete self-absorption reveals how much I have missed these two realities: the holiness of God and the depravity of humankind. *I have grossly underestimated my sin.* My idolatry, my unending quest to create and sustain my own reputation, is the evidence that convicts me in heaven's courts. I care about my reputation because *I think I am God.*

Satan, the accuser, tells me that God has treated me poorly. At that point he's not accusing me, he's accusing God in my thoughts. He is feeding my obsession with self-pity. The lie says, *"You wanted God but He didn't want you, you poor misunderstood victim."* Every argument for "fairness" is built on that lie.

The truth is, God wanted us but we didn't want Him!

The question, "What is fair?" waits patiently for an answer.

◊ ◊ ◊

Each of us has a list of what we consider fair and unfair.

Someone you know has lived a hedonist lifestyle, doing anything he pleases (some of those things you are envious of). He is dying, and with his last breath he utters sincere words of repentance, puts his trust in Jesus, dies, and goes to heaven. That's not fair. He got to do all the fun stuff you wish you could do—but know is wrong—and then when he's too old and too sick to do that stuff, he repents and goes to heaven. Grossly unfair. That's what I thought as a lost young man who felt like religion was robbing me of all the fun.

One child is brilliant. That's fair if that's my child. But this child is also undisciplined—and that's not fair.

That man is a millionaire because he works hard. That's fair. That other guy is a millionaire because his daddy was a millionaire, and the boy is a lazy, loud bully. That's not fair.

So fairness seems too fickle, too hard to pin down. What is fair?

I remember another class and another day. I was a visiting lecturer at a private parochial school in Dallas, Texas. I had just read John 14 to the class, in which Jesus said, "I am the way and the truth and the life. No one comes to the Father except through me" (v. 6).

"Jesus is the only One who can bring us to God," I began.

This time it was a guy who stood up at the back of the class. "That is so narrow minded!" Everyone turned to see who was speaking.

He continued, "How can you possibly say that Jesus is the only way to God, when there are many sincere Muslims, Hindus, and Jews who find God without Jesus?" The boy went on. "Don't get me wrong—I believe Jesus was good, the Son of God, and that He died for my sins and maybe even rose from the dead. But all this talk about Him being the only way to God seems too unfair to me. What about all the pagans in Africa who've never even heard of Jesus?"

Definitely a "fairness" question. I hope I thanked him for his courage. I don't remember.

"Let me see if I understand you correctly," I replied. "What you are saying is this: 'God, thank You for sending Your Son to earth as a man. Thank You, Jesus, for living like a man, letting people humiliate You even though You were kind to them. Thanks for letting them spit on You and curse You and beat You. You even let them hang You on a cross where You died for all of our sins. It was nice of You, nice but not necessary. You see, I believe that if we are all basically good people and try to do right, it doesn't matter what we believe about You. The important thing is that we need to be sincere, and if we are sincere, we will be okay."

I looked at the rest of the class, "What you are really saying is this: *'God, You made a terrible mistake!* You thought the *only* way I could get to be with You was through the sacrifice and death of Your only Son Jesus, but I found another way to You. Another hundred ways. God, You sacrificed Jesus unnecessarily. You were a horrible father!'

The classroom was very quiet.

Maybe the world needs to be quiet.

God didn't make a terrible mistake. He isn't a horrible father. Our only way to get to God is through the death and resurrection of Jesus. Our demands for "fairness" as we define it betray our heart's view of God. We have placed ourselves on thrones looking out over the kingdom of God and we have passed judgment on the King of eternity, time, and space. How extraordinarily absurd! We correct God, insisting that life go the way we want.

Fair is whatever the King does. *Fair* is who God *is*. I need to throw away my list of what is fair and make a new list. Whatever God does, who God reveals Himself to be, that's what goes on my new list. This is the definition of *fair*.

The good news starts right here, with our view of God and ourselves. But it is only good news to those who believe the bad news. If a man is drowning but doesn't know it, a rope thrown to him will make no sense to him. But if he knows the bad news—that he is about to go under for the third time—he will eagerly grasp for the rope.

When we minimize our sin, we minimize the cross. We argue for fairness, but the only fair response to our sin would be our eternal judgment in hell. God went beyond fair and gave us mercy. But take another look at mercy and justice. When you hear someone ask, "What would you rather have, justice or mercy?" wait until everyone finishes shouting "Mercy," and then gently shout "Justice" and turn to 1 John 1:9: "If we confess our sins, he is faithful and *just* to forgive us our sins and to cleanse us from all unrighteousness" (ESV).

Because of God's justice we have forgiveness! Because of God's justice, we have mercy. It isn't because God was so softhearted, as though pity was a good enough reason to forgive sins. Jesus satisfied the legal requirements of God's law. Maybe we should stop demanding fair and start receiving this amazing grace of God.

So again I face the reality that my pursuit of my own will, my own reputation, and my own understanding of fairness is a rejection of God, His will, His reputation, and true fairness. And God is gracious to forgive my sin.

◊ ◊ ◊

And then the curtain opens and lights come up,
all eyes are focused on us, and in the rush of that
first burst of applause, we remember. . . .

in pursuit of glory

"Before there was a before or after, before time filled space and defined creation, there was One."

emember looking around to see if anyone saw you make that jump shot in your driveway—"Nothing but net!"—or Mom's video of you twirling around in your butterfly costume in that kindergarten play? All of us long for glory. We have pursued it from childhood until this moment. *But we don't know whether to deny, confess, or celebrate this longing!*

Just a short list of older reality TV shows like *Star Search*, *American Idol* (if ever a show could claim divine inspiration for its title, this show is it!), or, for an earlier generation, the sitcom-turned-Broadway-musical *Fame* reflects our interest in stardom and glory.

Clothing styles follow the fashion of the stars, hair styles reflect the latest look from Hollywood. The cosmetic industry is awash in the smells of celebrity. We are star struck!

This isn't anything new. It seems to have increased in intensity due to media overload, but one generation is as guilty as the next. (Ask your mom why she wears her glasses on top of her head. Maybe she has no idea, or maybe she'll confess she first saw Farah Fawcett introducing this look in a shampoo commercial a generation ago.)

God speaks directly to the subject of the pursuit of glory, and we might be surprised at what He has to say.

We were designed for glory. We were "wired" for glory by God Himself—it was part of being made in His image.

Humankind knew this glory once. God explains what happened next: "For all have sinned and fall short of the glory of God" (Romans 3:23). We have devoted ourselves to trying to recover that glory, all the while clinging to the sin that caused our fall from glory.

Do we want the glory without the God of glory? This is an insurmountable problem. We pursue all forms of counterfeit glory. We perform our hearts out for the applause of an audience, the "fifteen minutes of fame" Andy Warhol said was our due. But fifteen minutes doesn't seem like enough. I read somewhere that Woody Allen said, "I don't want to be famous, I want immortality!" The recognition that comes with being the "best" in our sport, business, art, and ministry—this is what we insist on. This is what we get up in the morning for.

For those people who have experienced some measure of stardom, pressure comes with fame. It is often said that the curse of show business is that whatever success you achieve, it is never enough. Charlton Heston, best known as "Moses," once remarked in a now-yellowed newspaper interview that all actors live fearful lives. When they are acting, they are afraid it won't last. When they are not working, they are afraid they will never work again. They are afraid that people won't like their work anymore. They may be easily replaced by someone younger, better, more beautiful. As one producer told me at a poolside party, "Record company A&R people are looking for three things in a future star. They have to be *young, beautiful*, and *talented*, and the talent part is negotiable." When you are immersed in the world of acting, music, and art, it is impossible to escape this kind of attitude from others.

Whatever our environment, we are never satisfied with being good at something. We insist on comparing ourselves with others and being recognized as better than they are. The Pharisee looks at the tax collector in Luke 18 and says, "God, I thank you that I am not like other men" (v. 11).

A privilege comes with success, though, and it is addictive. I have told successful performers, "There is nothing wrong with being treated as a 'star.' It's normal if people appreciate your work and ask for autographs or want to be seen with you. You didn't insist on it; at first you were even embarrassed by it. The problem comes when you *expect* to be treated as a 'star.'"

Privilege becomes a right, and rights become needs, and booking agents insist on contracts that require "star treatment." This is true for athletes or recording artists or senior pastors.

But those who have never received this kind of glory are envious, secretly longing for it and often quick to pass judgment on those who have it. We examine the lives of the successful with a microscope, looking for failure to pounce on so we can assuage our underachieving conscience. *If I can't make myself better than that guy, maybe I can cut him down to my size by finding his flaws. Then I'll feel better about myself.* Occasionally those of us who've been doing the "pouncing and cutting" stumble into some measure of personal fame and then suffer the same scrutiny and judgment we've been guilty of showing others. We are indignant and hurt—and hopefully learning important lessons about humility.

For some husbands (probably many more than we imagine), the pursuit of glory had everything to do with their pursuit of a beautiful woman to marry. Some call her a "trophy wife." If she is beautiful, people will think, *You must be an important person if she wanted to marry you.* (Implied is the uncomfortable assumption that you are nothing to write home about without her.) While Cinderella is flattered by that attention, she wonders what she will do when the clock strikes midnight and the beauty wanes.

And women may be surfing the talent-net looking for a man whose success in business or financial savvy will make her look good. So we pursue glory for wrong reasons and with wrong means. Since it's impossible to succeed this way, we fail and fail again.

What do we do then? We get mad and we look for a way to dull the pain of our failure, or we try other false means of attaining glory.

Do you remember that boy I wrote about earlier, who boasted and showed off to find a reason for being? I wanted glory but it was a false glory, and it was never enough.

◊ ◊ ◊

Years ago I worked in Canyon, Texas, as a Campus Crusade staff member at the university there. My roommate was also my director; we were the only staff there.

John was from Nebraska, like me.

He had been a music major, like me.

He was a believer and on staff with CCC, like me.

With all of that in common how could we miss, right?

Wrong.

Relating to John was like trying to hit a slow hanging curve ball. I swung at it about a hundred times and missed by a mile every time.

John was organized. I was creative.

John lined his shoes up perfectly in his closet. My left shoe had been lost for a week and I didn't even know it.

John was quiet. I was loud.

John was disciplined. I was confessing a lot.

It's sort of like years later when Gail and I went through a series of psychological tests in order to join our mission.

We sat down with the psychologist and he looked at the test results and then looked up at Gail and announced: "Good news, Gail—you are normal!"

Great! Now where do you go from there? Too late to get out.

I laughed and looked at Gail, but my laugh was nervous. She laughed, but her laugh was normal.

I sat there, squirming a bit in my chair, feeling as if I had just been sent to the principal's office and waiting for the bad news (an experience not at all unfamiliar to me).

The psychologist looked over at me. I think he laughed but I can't remember. "Paul," he said, "you are *colorful!*" Whew. It could have been worse, right?

Well, John was certainly normal and my "colorful" didn't connect at all with that. So I would show off, thinking he might notice and think I was normal too. But it didn't have the effect I wanted. You see, John didn't like show-offs, and he had a built-in way of dealing with guys like me. He ignored them.

One time I came home from campus boasting about a fraternity president who'd responded to the gospel with me and just become a Christian. Now anybody in Christian work would think that is good news. But the way I announced it proved I was looking for glory. John's response was to go into his room, close the door, and read his Bible. He ignored me. I assumed he just didn't notice, so I showed off a little more, and he ignored me a little more. I would boast a little more . . . You can see where this is going. It was a long year for both of us.

(God does work in proud hearts like mine and John's. We both confessed to God that we were doing a poor job of loving unconditionally and by the end of the year we had learned a lot about how to love like Jesus loves us. When Gail and I were married two years later, John was a gracious member of our wedding party.)

Not everybody is impressed with our pursuit of personal glory, are they? Neither is God. But His response is different. Instead of moving away from us, He moves toward us. He reminds us that we were made for glory. True glory—a glory that comes from the Father of glory. But we don't find glory by seeking glory. We find it by seeking God. And we are not so far from experiencing that truth as we might think.

◊ ◊ ◊

Our roots of "reputation building" always seem to snake through our pursuit of glory, but God has a surprise for pretenders like you and me. . . .

*"It's laughter
of delight
from the
One, holy
and true."*

CHAPTER 9

the pretenders

uring the Soviet years, workers in factories, frustrated
with living and working conditions under their party
bosses, had a saying: "You pretend to pay us, we pretend to
work."

One of the most common excuses people use when
they decline an invitation to church is, "There are too many
hypocrites—too many pretenders—there." Of course they
are right, though our first inclination is to deny the accusation. Maybe we would be better off to agree and ask, "If
God is any kind of God, do you think He knows this? And
do you think He can help 'pretenders' too? I certainly hope
so—I'm one of the worst sometimes!"

At least two variations of pretenders are in the church.
The most well-known and most preached about are the
hypocrites. In Jesus's day the hypocrites were often the
Pharisees, teachers of the law, and the Sadducees. They
pretended to be devout lovers of God. But Jesus saw through
their pretensions and called them "whitewashed tomb-

stones." They were beautiful on the outside but inside they
were "full of dead people's bones" (Matthew 23:27 ESV).

These are the people Jesus faced on the way to the
cross. These are the people who mocked, argued, slan-
dered, beat, and eventually crucified Him. These pretenders
were enemies of Christ and His church. They still are. And
they are still in the church. They are orphans, pretending to
be sons or daughters.

But there is another type of pretender in the church. The
sons and daughters pretending they are still orphans.

When the voices of the enemy assault us they say, *"You
are such a hypocrite. You are only pretending to love God."*
And we believe. *I am such a two-faced person, I hate myself.
I don't love God. I never want to be with Him.* We repeat
the lies word for word as we heard them from our enemy.
And we find it to be a short step from Satan's accusations
and condemnation to drowning in self-pity. It's amazing
how long we can stay down there and drag everyone
around us down too.

The problem with this pretending is that it begins with a
measure of the truth. If I had a "life verse," it might come
from Romans chapter 7: "I do not understand what I do."
(An amazing thing for the apostle Paul to say—he seemed
to understand everything. Everything but himself.) "For what
I want to do I do not do, but what I hate I do" (v. 15). And
we stop reading, close our Bibles, and say with a melan-
choly honesty, "That's right. I'm such a phony, such a
pretender."

We all feel like this at times. This pretension immobilizes
us with a kind of fated, subtle self-righteousness. We assume
that transparency equals repentance and we can't change
ourselves anyway because our addictions are insurmount-

able (which is a problem, because we are all addicted to something, whether it's control or praise or food or . . .). But we are strangely smug in our pseudo confession: *I'm such a hypocrite sometimes.*

I know a man who struggles mightily with addiction. He attends help sessions every day, sometimes twice a day. He has little joy and no freedom. He has a great heaviness about him; it seems his only hope is in heaven to come. He told me that his friends in these help sessions call him Pity Me.

Who needs help like that? Give a guy a label and then ask him to hope for change? People like this guy might say, "I'll always be like this, so if I am unable to change, at least I can attempt to atone for it with a modest honesty."

Impossible.

But there is a difference between this pretender and the ones like the Pharisees of Jesus' day. This individual is a genuine Christian. This pretender is a son "pretending" to be an orphan! Ask him, "Are you a sinner or a saint?" and without hesitation he would say, "Sinner."

And if we opened the curtain on our own acting we would be surprised at what we would see.

The truth is that we really are "new creations" (2 Corinthians 5:17 FSV). We really are "crucified with Christ" as Paul writes in Galatians: "It is no longer I who live, but Christ who lives in me. And the life I now live in the flesh I live by faith in the Son of God, who loved me and gave himself for me" (2:20 ESV).

But this son acting like an orphan might protest, "If you only knew how I struggle with my temptations." And this protest reveals his real struggle—the struggle to believe God.

If we pulled back the curtain a little further in ourselves, we would see Satan back there whispering, shouting, and cursing at us: *"You are such a fake, you are never going to change. Not even God can change you!"* He snarls and laughs. And we hang our heads in shame.

But we stopped reading too soon in Romans 7. Finish out Paul's confession in verse 17: "As it is, it is no longer I myself who do it, but it is sin living in me."

Someone interrupts Paul to say, "So you don't sin anymore? You never sin once you become a Christian? The devil made you do it; it's not your fault?"

But that is not what Paul is saying. In fact, he refers to himself as a "wretched man" (v. 24). He can say what he does about sin because of the truths in the beginning of chapter 7.

Somebody died.

It was us—we who believe in Jesus.

"Who will rescue me from this body of death? Thanks be to God, through Jesus Christ our Lord!" (vv. 24–25).

When Jesus died on the cross for our sins, we died too. When He rose from the grave to new life, we rose too. And in our death and resurrection we were set free from the law, which had condemned us to hell.

Paul goes on to assure us of this only a few verses later in 8:1: "Therefore, there is now no condemnation for those who are in Christ Jesus." Notice that Paul doesn't say "Therefore, there is now no need for forgiveness for those who are in Christ Jesus." We still need forgiveness, but without condemnation. We are, in our flesh, wretched.

So which is it, Paul: Are you or are you not wretched? Yes!

"But it is no longer I myself who do it. . . ." Once but no longer. Theologians refer to this paradox as the "already and not yet." It is already true and not yet fully realized.

We often forget the "already" and surrender to the "not yet." When we stop hoping, we have given in to the voices of the enemy.

God knew we wouldn't be able to get our arms around this truth easily, so He told Paul to write those exact words again: "Now if I do what I do not want to do, it is no longer I who do it, but it is sin living in me that does it" (Romans 7:20). Do you see? Twice, He tells us the same thing. He knows how hard it is for us to believe this!

The key to understanding this has to do with the "want" and the "no longer." If I want to do the sin, I'm still doing it. But if, in my heart, I'm divided over it—part of me wants to and part of me doesn't—what can that mean but that I'm not the one doing it any longer? That is, the new me is not doing it—the real me from heaven's perspective.

This is the "truest" me. I hate it when I give in to temptation. I despise those times when I let sin "reign in my mortal body." I'm ashamed of my boasting.

I've changed. I still boast sometimes, but I've changed.

So who is pretending? I am. How am I pretending? When I sin, I hear the voices that say, *"This is the real you, Paul."* And I nod my head in numb agreement. I'm pretending to still be lost. I'm pretending that nothing has changed within me.

Am I a new creation or am I not? This is the battle to be fought. Will I believe what God says about me, or will I believe Satan's voices, the father of lies, telling me that God couldn't change me?

◊ ◊ ◊

In Peter's first letter he writes about God's "call" on your life and my life. In the first chapter, verses 15–16, we read:

"But just as he who called you is holy, so be holy in all you do; for it is written, 'Be holy, because I am holy.'"

Oh, is that all?

The church reads these verses and lets out a collective sigh of discouragement. "It's impossible." Our heads drop and we shuffle away defeated before the battle has begun.

But actually the battle is already underway—we just weren't listening when somebody said, "Go." We are already facing an enemy.

What is our offensive weapon? "The sword of the Spirit, which is the word of God" (Ephesians 6:17).

But, I sin so much. That is my experience.

So, you and I have a choice. Will we believe our "experience" or will we believe God's Word? Which is truer? Will we use our weapon or lay it down in surrender?

Look back at the impossible command in Peter's letter. Did you notice the wording?

"Be holy, because I told you to be holy," right?

Try again.

"Be holy because it's the right thing to do," right?

Try again.

Listen to it carefully: *"Be holy because I am holy."*

We interrupt, and our frustration grows. *But how can I be holy just because You are? You are God; I am not.*

And God patiently but with great enthusiasm says, "Yes! You've got it!"

Got what?

God smiles. "You are to be who you are. You are designed for glory. You have been made new in My image, holy, like Jesus, filled with His righteousness, not your own. You are holy because I am holy. Be who you are!"

First Peter 1:15–16 is a promise as much as it is a

command. We, who are new creatures, have been hidden in Christ. We are to make choices not as if our new status will someday be true, but because it is now, already true. We live out of the truth, not just toward it.

Be holy. It's who you and I are. Are you sinner or saint? Amazingly, the answer is saint. This is the grace of God.

And with one final protest we say, "But what about Paul writing to the church in Philippi: 'Not that I have already obtained all this, or have already been made perfect.' (Philippians 3:12). See, it's not yet true of me."

But wait.

I am not already holy in my effort, my obtaining "all this." I am holy because of what Jesus has done. What He did was enough to satisfy the holy God.

Paul wrote to the church at Corinth: "He made him [Jesus] to be sin who knew no sin, so that in him we might become the righteousness of God" (2 Corinthians 5:21 ESV).

If Jesus took all of our sin, then we, who receive this sacrifice by believing in Him, must also receive all of His righteousness.

Be holy. *It's the truest thing about you.* When you pray, you are doing what comes naturally now. When you tell the truth, this is your new "native language." When you say no to temptations to "get even" with someone, you are doing nothing extraordinary; it's the normal choice of a thoroughly transformed nature. Believe it!

I remember what I prayed and wrote in my journal years ago:

Thank You, Lord, for these thoughts and prayers. Even in the darkness of unknowing and the fearful-ness of knowing too much, I see You. In the dread of willful habits, I still hear something that sounds like hope coming from Your heart. And in the delight of choices well made, I hear You say, "This is the truest thing about you!" I am "more than a conqueror"; I am a son, a child of God, a child of Yours, Father. Constantly accused by the enemy, condemned by the demons of hell, I cry out to You for truth.

But strength builds inside me as the truth is thrown down alongside the lie. For the truth exposes the lie, sucking the life out of it!

And my voice and pen are stopped and my ears stopped up and a silent cry echoes in my head like the sound of an ocean and I am somewhere between heaven and earth though much closer to heaven. Time stands still and my senses are given over to a "feeling of being" I wish would never stop—I am in Your presence and nothing is better and nothing more fearful—all truths are weighed in that moment, all doubts suspended and You are God.

This is the grace of God, brothers and sisters! The truth about Jesus defines the truth about us, and suddenly our own glory and failures are nothing in the light of His face.

◊ ◊ ◊

And perhaps we are now ready, with confidence, to venture in to the Holy of Holies, by the blood of Jesus, and see what no one can see and live. . . .

the one

Before there was a before or after, before time filled space and defined creation, there was One. Not at all someone short or tall, waiting or hurrying, early or late. No time or space or words could tame the One powerful to create yet wise to transcend those limitations.

The One was beyond anything the senses suspect—infinitely.

Beyond everything but revelation. Beauty was the anticipation of His face. Integrity, a reflection in His eyes, the bluest sky shining in the clearest pond.

The One had no audience, no need for an audience. Everything that is life, and good, everything that is beautiful, delicious, and compelling, alive forever within the One! Three yet One, He was never lonely. Never anxious. Never surprised, yet never bored, that alone must be some kind of definition of deity. Before the beginning was the One. . . .

And then came the many. Not before, or after, not instead of the One, but because of the One: the many. Yet however many there could be, the sum total of their energy and ideas, their dreams and passions, the sum total of their existence forgotten in an instant with one fraction of a glimpse of the One.

The One is beyond imagining, but many imagine. Beyond seeing, yet many somehow see. All attempts to paint and sculpt, to compose His likeness, lie incomplete, inspired dust. Yet the many create because they must. What is that sound? Heaven? Laughing? Not mocking. Not condescending or smug. It's laughter of delight from the One, holy and true.

Every effort to know Him, to paint Him, to make Him known, all such thoughts and efforts conceived in His heart first. And Heaven laughs, and it's good! And songs are sung, poems read, and the many laugh and weep and should, imagine the One!

But the many wanted to be the One, and fell. . . .

The One searched the heavens and earth, time and space, to find a reason to love the many. He found none. He searched their hearts, and still no reason could be found. Finally, the One searched His own heart, and there He found all the reasons He could ever need to love the many.

It's all about the One. . . .

Every true prayer that's ever been prayed, every longing to embrace all that's good and right, and every love inspired by faith is a gift of grace to the many from the One. Past, present, and future find their reason for being in the One. Indeed, every breath breathed is about the One.

And the One is the One and Only,

And the many, of course, are only you and me.

*"But the
many
wanted to
be the
One,
and fell."*

a profound repentance

It had been four hundred years of silence. Four hundred years since God had sent a messenger to His people. Generations had lived and died. And then God spoke.

In the fifteenth year of Tiberius Caesar's reign, the Word of God came to John the son of Zechariah in the desert. The Holy Spirit had prepared Israel for this moment. In the book of Malachi we read a prophecy about John: "Behold, I send my messenger and he will prepare the way before me" (Malachi 3:1 ESV). What will this messenger do to "prepare the way"? What would he say?

If you were silent for four days would anyone notice? How about silent for four weeks or months or even four years?

We remember the first word our children speak. For months they cried and pointed to what they wanted and tried out new sounds, and then the day came when that first word was spoken and we ran into the other room to drag a spouse or sister or brother in to hear. Of course, the baby looked at us as though we were interrupting playtime and said nothing. But we celebrated that first word.

What if our child waited forty years before speaking? Would we take notice? Absolutely. Would we remember her first word? Of course we would.

God was silent for four hundred years! Do we want to know what He said, what He waited so long to tell us?

John went into all the region around the Jordan proclaiming a baptism of repentance for the forgiveness of sins (Matthew 3:1–2, my paraphrase).

"Repentance for the forgiveness of sins." That was the message that could no longer wait to be told. My greatest need is relationship with my Father in heaven, and repentance is the door to that intimacy.

John was preparing the way for Jesus—Jesus, who'd had all of eternity past to prepare His first sermon. What did Jesus leave heaven's glory to say to the prisoners of time and space? Would he begin by asking us what we thought of Him? Would He announce the return of Israel's splendor?

"From that time Jesus began to preach, saying 'Repent, for the kingdom of heaven is at hand'" (Matthew 4:17 ESV).

"Repent!" The same message John the Baptist began with. Jesus tells us He only taught what His Father told Him to teach, so these words were from our Father.

The irony is that this was one message Jesus knew nothing about, not by personal experience. He never needed to repent—not ever. So He spoke not from experience but from observation and revelation. He saw our need, and God spoke.

But we are often confused about what true repentance looks like. Is the call to repent merely a scolding to work harder at being good? Is it an order to stop doing some things and start doing other things?

It is much more profound than that and much lighter than that. It is a call to come to God as I am. Only God can change me. To repent is to admit I can't fix myself and to enter into ongoing relationship with my Father not on the basis of my reputation but because of the reputation of Jesus.

Is it possible that the church today desperately needs the message of repentance? Why do we remain slaves of sin after giving our hearts to Christ? Why are we mired in habits generations deep and see no way out?

Perhaps we have practiced a "selective repentance" rather than a "profound repentance."

Should I begin by repenting of my poor repenting?

◊ ◊ ◊

Look at the reluctant prophet Jeremiah. (God often chooses reluctant people, like Moses or Gideon, to deliver powerful messages.) God says in Jeremiah 1, "Whatever I command you, you shall speak" (v. 7 ESV). And, "Behold, I have put my words in your mouth" (v. 9 ESV). And what are the words God put in Jeremiah's mouth?

The heart of God's message is revealed in chapter 2, verse 13: "For my people have committed two evils: they have forsaken me, the fountain of living waters, and hewed out cisterns for themselves, broken cisterns that can hold no water" (ESV).

Does this mean Israel committed only two evils? Even a casual reading of Judges will reveal many more than two evils. So what does God mean?

God is giving us a principle. He tells us that Israel's sins are grouped in two general categories. The second group is comprised of all the surface sins, such as lying, lust, coveting, cursing, stealing, selfishness, and vanity. It also includes sins like pride that cause surface sins. These are the cisterns—the broken cisterns that can hold no water, the sins of trying to make life work in our own ways with our own strength. These are the "second" sins, the second evil.

So what is the first evil? "They have forsaken me, the fountain of living waters." The first sin is the sin of rejecting God. This is always the first sin. When I sin, I always sin twice. A root sin comes first, leading to surface sins—an invisible sin that leads to a visible sin.

And the first sin is always the worst sin. Always. Why?

The first sin is our rejection of God's right to be God. It is our idolatry. We exchange the true God for a false god, a god who is really no god at all.

Nearly every major and minor book of the Prophets tells us of God's promised judgment for the sin of idolatry. But is it only a sin of Israel? Do we have little Baals hidden in our closets?

We who love Jesus and want so much to please Him are idolaters, too, and we often forget this first sin. We are quick to repent and grieve over the second sins—we hate our addictions to gluttony or anxiety. We loathe our hateful words and our hair-trigger temper. We confess these sins again and again. And it's right to confess and repent of these sins.

Yet they return to enslave us. Many times I want to throw my hands up and resign myself to this pattern, assuming that's the way life is until heaven.

At the risk of oversimplifying, perhaps one reason we are such repeat offenders is because we only confess the surface. We go through our garden plucking off the tops of weeds, removing all visible evidence of sin but ignoring the roots. I imagine my sins against others to be huge but have forgotten what my sins do to our Holy God and Loving Father. I have not stopped to repent of rejecting the One who has made me, who holds my next breath in His hands.

◊ ◊ ◊

Consider David. You may have heard of his sins before, but have you ever connected his story to issues of reputation? Look again. An innocent son of Jesse who trusted God. The boy who was too small to wear a man's armor but threw caution to the wind and stones at giants. The shepherd boy who sang and wrote "hit songs" like, "The Lord is my shepherd, I shall not be in want. He makes me lie down in green pastures . . . he restores my soul" (Psalm 23:1–3). How could this happen to a man whom God Himself describes as "a man after my own heart" (Acts 13:22)? But it did.

How far would you go to protect your reputation? Would you work eighty-hour weeks and abandon your children and spouse? Or say whatever people want you to say and laugh at jokes that you disciplined your son for telling? Would you lie on your résumé in order to secure the head coaching job of a major football power? Would you plagiarize speeches in order to win political office, or fabricate sources and stories in order to fill columns for your *New York Times* readers?

David, king of Israel, poet and prophet, man after God's own heart. How far would he go to protect his reputation?

He was caught. His reputation as God's leader was in jeopardy. He had stolen another man's wife and now she was pregnant.

But kings can't get on the next bus out of town and

become taxi drivers five hundred miles away. No, kings are on top of the world, more visible than anyone. Kings have to be more clever. Or more devious.

How far would you go to protect your reputation?

David would rather kill someone than repent publicly and endure the shame of his acts. David was willing to lie and deceive in order to protect his image as "God's man."

And when his deceptions and manipulations failed because of Uriah's strength of character, he exercised his right as king and ordered a general to put this brave and loyal soldier in harm's way, guaranteeing his death in battle. But David is not alone in his desire to protect his image.

◊ ◊ ◊

When I was a new believer, about eighteen years old, I cheated on a final exam project in college. I was supposed to turn in three hundred note cards. Each card represented research in the library, but I wasn't even sure where the library was, so I copied someone else's work. Nearly everyone in the class did the same thing.

But I'm certain no one went through what I went through.

Having turned in my plagiarized cards at the last possible moment, I slithered back to my fraternity house dragging my guilt behind me. I couldn't eat, I couldn't sleep. If I tried to pray, my thoughts were cluttered with shame, and I couldn't think about anything else. The Holy Spirit was convicting my heart. This was still a new experience for me and I didn't care much for it. I was groaning inside but afraid to repent.

The problem was that my professor was also the wrestling coach. If you recall, I was a wrestler. Okay, not a great one, but I loved it and the coach knew me. He knew me before I became a Christian. After I gave my life to Jesus, the changes in me were so obvious that this coach came to me and said, "Paul, why don't you tell some of the other wrestlers what happened to you? Maybe it will help them too." They were a rowdy bunch of guys.

Now, a new Christian, I was afraid to confess my sin because my reputation was on the line. This was why I couldn't bear to admit my cheating. But I couldn't bear the guilt either. Finally the convicting work of the Holy Spirit broke through my need to protect my reputation. I asked God for forgiveness and then went to see the coach.

"Coach, I need to tell you something. I cheated on those cards we turned in for class. I copied them from another student."

He said exactly what I feared he would say. "Paul, I thought you were a Christian," and he could hardly suppress his smile. "How could you do something like this?"

"Coach," I replied, "this is why I became a Christian. I'm such a mess and I need a Savior."

He was so taken aback by my honesty he didn't know what to do. He then offered me an opportunity to save my grade in the class (grace from God and a godless professor), which required that I introduce myself to the library and live there for a couple of days. I got a B in the class but deserved far worse.

Something else happened. For the rest of my college days, that tough wrestling coach could hardly look me in the eyes. I realized he was afraid of me. Amazing. I let go of my reputation for the sake of an honest repentance and God made His reputation in me one hundred times stronger as far as that coach was concerned. My coach feared a holy God who could change someone that much. But I still had much to learn from King David.

David had committed adultery with Bathsheba. After their child was born, the baby became very ill and died. How long did it take David—"a man after God's own heart"—to repent? A week? A month?

It was about a year before David dealt honestly with his sin. A year of carrying all that stuff around inside. And then David decided to repent, right?

No.

No?

Not even after nearly twelve months of groaning.

So God helped him by sending Nathan the prophet to him. (This is a great example of grace in the Old Testament). The kindness of God (Romans 2) led to repentance then too.

But even after all that time, repentance was very hard for a proud man like David. Reputation is a terrible idol in our hearts, which can demand even murder as a sacrifice on its altar.

◊ ◊ ◊

We can learn some important lessons about repentance by listening to David.

Psalm 32 describes how David felt as the Holy Spirit worked inside his mind and heart even before Nathan was sent to him. "For day and night your hand was heavy upon me; my strength was sapped as in the heat of summer" (v. 4). (That was exactly how I felt after cheating on the exam!)

But true repentance is more than a feeling of remorse. David says he "groaned all day long" (see v. 3). He felt terrible about his sin; he never stopped groaning about it, but that wasn't enough to make him want to repent. If it were, then God would never have needed to send the prophet Nathan to him.

You and I groan over our sins but it doesn't change our hearts or our behavior. True repentance changes our practice, changes the way we look at sin, but first and foremost it turns our attention away from ourselves and onto Jesus. David's groaning was a false repentance—he was still focused on himself.

One way you can recognize a false repentance is to ask this question, "Am I willing to tell God my sin but unwilling to let others hear my confession?" If I'm still trying to protect myself from what others think, then maybe I'm not repenting sincerely. Listen to what David wrote as he looked back on this time: "Blessed is the man . . . in whose spirit is no deceit" (Psalm 32:2).

False repentance covers up, hides its sin from others. It blame-shifts and defends itself. Does this mean we should take out a full page ad in *Time* magazine or *The Wall Street Journal* to announce our repentance? Of course not. But it does mean we allow those close to us, who will listen without condemning us, to hear our honest confession. It means we are willing to put our reputation on the line, and say, "I hate my sin. But I have a Savior and, by the way, I need a Savior more than you can imagine."

Notice something else in David's song. It's a surprise. "Therefore let everyone who is godly pray" (Psalm 32:6).

Did you see it? Did you get the surprise?

I didn't either, not even after years of reading. And then one day it jumped off the page. "Therefore" insists that there is a correlation between everything that comes before it and everything that follows.

If I were writing this psalm, I would have said, "There-fore, let anyone who is ungodly pray, confess like this." After all, repentance is for the ungodly, isn't it?

We sometimes forget that repentance is for the godly too. In fact, David may be re-defining godliness for us here. The godly are not those who never sin. Only Jesus would qualify. No, the godly person is the person who hates sin, knows how to repent, and repents from a sincere heart.

But David isn't through teaching me. I turn to Psalm 51 (I'm sure some of you knew we'd have to look here). Here, David truly repents. He owns his sin, describing it in vari-ous terms as though he's saying, "I don't want you to miss this. What I did was

sin,

iniquity,

transgression,

evil."

You see here no attempt to hide or cover up. In fact, the opposite is true. He says, "If you think this is bad, I was born in sin." Then he reconsiders and says, "No, that's not bad enough. The fact is I was conceived in sin."

All of us are sinners by nature, by conception, because of Adam and Eve. This fact more than anything else exposes the hopelessness of our best reputation-building efforts. We don't start out innocent. We don't begin with a clean slate.

Now David's confession goes to a place few of us know. Listen carefully, as though we overhear his private conver-sation with God. "Against you, you only, have I sinned and done what is evil in your sight" (Psalm 51:4).

And heaven shakes and angels burst into praise of our Holy God. Hell is shaken too for different reasons, terrified at a deep truth brought into the light.

And I'm flying at thirty-six thousand feet as I write this and the people on either side of me are oblivious to the tears I'm trying to hold back. And I'm with You, God. This plane can't possibly catch up to where my heart is soaring. You are God and I am not. How You surprise us with Your wonderful presence.

Listen again to David. "Against you, you only, have I sinned." If you listen carefully you hear other voices, voices in protest. Out of a grave a voice sounds—it's Uriah the Hittite and husband of Bathsheba: "David, what do you mean you only sinned against God? What about me? My life was cut short after you stole my wife and my life. How can you say you only sinned against God?"

Before this anger has a chance to subside we hear another voice, a woman's voice. "David, this is your wife Bathsheba. You took me by force into your bed and defiled me. Who can resist the king's command? But even if I were willing, I never wanted Uriah murdered! And I blamed myself. How can you say you only sinned against God? What about me? Didn't you sin against me?" Silence falls on her bewildered cry.

And in the silence yet another voice, not so strong and not so confident. A voice speaking for the first time. "Papa, what about me? You didn't even want to admit you were my father. You tried to trick Uriah into thinking I was his son. Because of your sin my life was counted in days, not years. How can you say you sinned only against God? Didn't you sin against me, Papa?"

The voices die down and return to their respective graves. And we hear David again, *"Against you, you only, have I sinned."* Heaven nods its head in solemn agreement. Again we hear God speaking through Jeremiah: *"My people have committed two evils. They have rejected me."*

And time is stopped and preachers everywhere are silent.

David's repentance in Psalm 51 is the perfect reminder of what God meant by the first sin in Jeremiah's book. David understood Jeremiah's word even though he came centuries before Jeremiah.

David saw that the worst thing about his sin was what it did to God. Yes, he sinned against Uriah, Bathsheba, and the infant. But he understood that when compared with his sin against God, his sin against them all but disappeared. He saw that the relationship we have with our invisible God takes precedence over our relationship with those we can see. Perhaps David's understanding of this truth is one reason why God called David a man after His own heart.

Consider Jesus's words in Luke 14: "If anyone comes to me and does not hate his father and mother, his wife and children . . ." (v. 26). Jesus, who told us that the greatest command is to love God and others, is not changing His mind and encouraging us to hate our family. His point is that our commitment to Him must be absolute and without comparison. All other loves look like hate when held up to the mirror of our loyalty to Jesus. All friends appear to be enemies compared to our relationship with Jesus.

This is what David means in Psalm 51. His sin against God is so foul, so uncalled for, so without excuse that all other offenses seem inconsequential.

Does God want us to repent before those people we offend? Yes.

Does He want us to set our reputation aside and admit our sins against others? Yes.

But the first sin is the worst. I can't continue to skip over it. I can't allow others to be more important to me than Jesus, and my offenses against them more offensive than my offenses against God.

So, this is it. A profound repentance. I must slow down, not be in such a hurry to put the memory of my sin behind me. God invites me to let Him forgive my sin against Him, let Him tell me how it hurt, how He felt.

He will forgive me, always, not because of a perfect repentance but because of a perfect Jesus.

◊ ◊ ◊

If the only reputation that matters is the One's,
how do I find Him to know His reputation,
His character, and His ways? I could learn
a lot from my son Nathaniel—and how
he used to play hide-and-seek. . . .

CHAPTER 11

hide-and-seek

When our son Nathaniel was about three years old, he loved to play hide-and-seek with his two big brothers. It was hard not to interfere with our sons when they played their hide-and-seek games. We could see how our older boys were taking advantage of their baby brother. But slowly the light began to dawn on these overprotective parents and we laughed and laughed.

Jon and Marty would say, "Hey Nathaniel, do you want to play hide-and-seek?"

And our three-year-old would get this big smile on his face and turn and run into some other part of the house to hide. Jon and Marty would count to ten or twenty out loud and then announce, "Ready or not, here we come."

Going from room to room they would wink at each other as they called out, "Nathaniel? Where are you?"

From under a bed or inside a closet they'd hear a tiny voice, "Here!" They'd lift the blanket or open the door and there would be Nathaniel with a big grin on his face. And they would laugh at their trick and then ask, "Do you want to play again?"

Little Nat would run and hide again as his big brothers counted and then announced, "Ready or not, here we come."

"Where are you Nathaniel?" they called out.

And of course the pattern repeated, the older brothers tricking Nat into giving away his hiding place. In their minds they had won the game. But the truth was that Nathaniel had won.

"How was that?" you ask. "Isn't the idea of the game to see if you can hide where nobody will think to look?"

But Nathaniel was playing a different game.

He wanted to be found. That was his goal all along. He wanted to be with his brothers. They were (and still are) his heroes.

He liked the idea of being pursued by his heroes.

◊ ◊ ◊

Can you imagine it? The one true God is our hero of heroes. He is the true pursuer, yet He is also the One who likes to be pursued by us. And He calls for us to find Him. It is not as though He is insecure and somehow needs us to search for Him. He wants it.

We read in Hebrews 11 that those who come to God "must believe that He is, and that He is a rewarder of those who seek Him" (11:6 NASB). How do the "people of the dark" who want to find God find Him in such blackness? How do I learn of who He is so I can promote His reputation and not my own?

The only way for us to know God is for Him to reveal Himself to us. *Revelation* is God showing us something about Himself we could not know unless He showed us. Theologians speak of two kinds of revelation: general and special.

General revelation is creation. It's you and me. It's the icebergs of the Arctic and the palm trees of the Caribbean. General revelation tells us there is a God. In Romans 1, Paul tells us that humankind has no excuse not to believe in God. This is general revelation.

But there is something that general revelation does not do. It does not tell us how to get to God. We know God is there because of nature. But we don't know how to have relationship with Him.

So the God who wants to be found has given us "special" revelation.

Special revelation is understood through God's Word and, most important, through His Son, Jesus. Through special revelation we learn how to get to God. We learn about His character. And we who seek Him find Him. This is the reward for those seeking Him.

But this reward doesn't always seem like enough to us, does it? I mean, if we are going to be honest, sometimes we sing along with Tevya as he looks up to heaven in the Broadway musical *Fiddler on the Roof* (the setting is in a pre-Bolshevik Ukraine), "If I were a rich man . . ."

"Why can't I be rich too, Lord?" we sing.

Do you remember Jesus telling us, "Ask and it will be given to you; seek and you will find; knock and the door will be opened to you" (Matthew 7:7)? The same words from Jesus are recorded in Luke 11. And in both passages the same analogy is used—a father giving good gifts to his son when he asks.

But there is a difference between Matthew and Luke in

how this passage ends. Matthew tells us, "If you, then, who are evil, know how to give good gifts to your children, how much more will your Father who is in heaven give good things to those who ask him!" (7:11 ESV).

I like this promise very much. The words "good things" intrigues me.

Is there a limit?

How much is too much?

Can I choose the style and color?

Is there a catch to it?

So I ask, seek, and knock, all the while looking for "good things" God has promised.

And then I read Luke's account of the same words from Jesus: "If you then, who are evil, know how to give good gifts to your children, how much more will the heavenly Father give the Holy Spirit to those who ask him!" (11:13 ESV).

And here is my confession; perhaps it's yours as well: there are times when I'm disappointed. I wanted the good things and all I got was the Holy Spirit. Sounds terrible, doesn't it?

It is.

Do you remember what we said before? We have grossly underestimated our sinful condition. The voices we hear convince us that the Holy Spirit is boring, a weak substitute. Our sin is in our believing the wrong messages: *"God is good, but not that good. God will give you 'spiritual stuff,' but you may go hungry in the meantime. You are lonely and need a husband so what does God offer you? A man? Oh no—He says He will give you Himself. Is that the best He can do? Sounds to me as if that's the spiritual equiv-alent of snakes for fish and scorpions for eggs. What kind of a pitiful God you must have. Maybe He only gives spiritual stuff because that's all He's got. There is no way for you to see that stuff, so how do you know if He's delivered it anyway? Maybe He isn't even good—maybe He isn't God at all."*

These voices of accusation, these lies and distortions, tell us not to seek God. They accuse God of not being good enough for us. Satan has done this from the Garden of Eden until now.

But once again we throw the truth down alongside the lie, and the lie is exposed and God is found again. "Finally . . . whatever is true . . . think about such things" (Philippians 4:8).

Again, the truth is that God wants us to seek Him, and He can be found.

"Seek the LORD while he may be found," Isaiah tells us. "Call on him while he is near" (Isaiah 55:6). God not only allows Himself to be discovered; His greatest longing is for us to find Him.

◊ ◊ ◊

So our time spent reading God's Word is like playing hide-and-seek with the One who wants to be discovered. But God's Word isn't like any other book. When we open the Bible, we come to a person. We come not for information, but for relationship with the One who stepped out of eternity and "made his dwelling among us" (John 1:14).

When I was younger in the faith, I first learned something about seeking the person of God when I was reading Psalm 119. I read in verse 9, "How can a young man keep his way pure?"

I was a young man, and I wanted to keep my way pure, so I was interested in the question. What was the answer?

"By living according to your word" (v. 9).

And then I read verse 11: "I have hidden your word in my heart that I might not sin against you."

This is perfect, I thought. It was the answer to my search for purity, so I "hid these words in my heart," memorizing them and drawing great encouragement from their truth. Then one day I was reading the psalm again and realized I had disregarded a basic principle of Bible study—I had ignored the context. I had skipped over the verse that came in between my two favorite verses.

So I read verse 10: "I seek you with all my heart."

How had I missed that?

God didn't want me to come to His Word simply as a means of fixing my broken life. He wanted me to come to a person—Him! He wanted me to come to listen. He wanted me to find Him! "I seek you with all my heart." This is the love of a Father for a child and a child for a Father.

God wants us to seek Him. When we stop asking where He is, we are no longer interested in the answer. Jeremiah tells us in 2:6, "They [Israel] did not ask, 'Where is the LORD?'" Again we see that the grace of God is in the questions, not only in the answers. We have permission to dialogue with Him, to ask Him hard questions. In fact, God *wants* us to ask Him hard questions.

So after we've counted out loud to about a million and announced, "Ready or not, here I come!" we finally ask, "Where are You, God?" And from under a blanket of clouds or behind a closed door we hear God say, "Here!" He is so patient with us. If He is laughing, it's the delight of having been found by us.

And when we find Him, what do we do? Sometimes we retreat, not ready yet to find our Father. Other times we want to run and jump into His arms, ready or not. And we look into the eyes of the One and Only and repent.

The profound repentance we looked at in chapter 9 comes after we find Jesus, not before. It's always been this way with the heroes of faith. When Isaiah found a holy God, he cried out, "Woe is me! For I am lost; for I am a man of unclean lips" (Isaiah 6:5 ESV). Job argued with God until God rebuked him, "Would you condemn me to justify yourself?" (Job 40:8). God reveals Himself and we hear this confession from Job in the last chapter: "I had heard of you by the hearing of the ear, but now my eyes see you; therefore I despise myself, and repent in dust and ashes" (42:5–6 ESV). Saul of Tarsus saw Jesus in a blinding light and this persecutor of the church repented. To see the One as He is causes me to see myself as I am, and I want to repent.

"Who are You, God?" Look into the eyes of our heavenly Father, who wants to be found by you, and you will see.

◊ ◊ ◊

Only the lonely seek God.

Jesus was the loneliest man to walk the face of the earth.

Jesus sought God the Father more than anyone has.

Do you believe those statements?

"Well, I believe your last statement, but I'm not sure about the first one, and no, I don't accept the second one, because Jesus had continual access to His Father, and besides, he was perfect. Perfect people can't be lonely."

I'm guessing your answers, of course, and I suppose they will vary from person to person.

Let's look first at the life of John the Baptist, a man who knew Jesus intimately. John had been imprisoned for telling King Herod that he was sinning by living with his brother's wife. All alone in prison he sends two of his disciples to ask Jesus, "Are you the one who is to come, or shall we look for another?" (Luke 7:19 ESV).

"But John!" we interrupt. "How can you, of all people, doubt that Jesus is the One? You recognized Jesus from inside your mama's womb! You were the voice crying in the wilderness, 'Prepare the way of the Lord,' and you baptized the Son of God. You heard the voice of God the Father watching from heaven, 'You are My Son whom I love, with you I am well-pleased.' He could no longer contain Himself, it was the cheer of a Father so proud of His Son. You saw the Spirit like a dove rest on Jesus. You told the people, 'Behold the Lamb of God,' 'I'm not worthy to tie His sandals,' 'He must increase, I must decrease.' Of all people, you can't have doubts, John!"

But John is lonely, lying on a cold, stinking floor on Herod's death row and he had doubts. (So would I.) Jesus is told about John's doubts. But Jesus doesn't rebuke him for struggling to believe. Instead, he sends John's disciples back with evidence that the prophecies of Isaiah are being fulfilled. He reminds him of God's promise, "Blessed is the man who does not fall away on account of me" (Luke 7:23). (Not "Cursed are you for doubting me, John.") Jesus offers truth to John to quiet the voices of doubt he is hearing in prison.

What do you do when you doubt if God is there? Run and hide, pretend you believe? Here's another choice. Do what John did. Go to Jesus with your doubts. It's okay; He already knows and still loves you.

So I was back home in Nashville, driving to Village Chapel for a Wednesday-night Bible study, and exhausted from trying to raise support for our ministry in Ukraine. After months of trying, it seemed hopeless to me, and finally I cried out to God. "I don't believe You, God. I don't believe You are going to raise the money I need. I have no faith in You for this; would you give us the money anyway?"

The next day Integrity Publishers called me and said they wanted to publish this book. Five days later I was on my way back to Kiev. I admitted I had no faith, yet He answered my prayer in a fantastic way. I came to Him as I was, unbelieving and weak, but still coming to Him.

Seeking God means coming to Him as we are, not as we should be. It means we trust God so much, that we will look for Him even though we are dragging our unbelief and failure behind us. God knows what to do with that stuff.

Look at an amazing example in the life of Jeremiah, the "weeping prophet." Here was a godly man wrestling with God over his pain. "O LORD, you deceived me, and I was deceived; you overpowered me and prevailed. I am ridiculed all day long; everyone mocks me. Whenever I speak, I cry out proclaiming violence and destruction. So the word of the LORD has brought me insult and reproach all day long" (Jeremiah 20:7–8).

When was the last time you called God a deceiver? No, I am not suggesting we should. I am suggesting that we do! The only difference between Jeremiah and us is that we only think these thoughts; Jeremiah says them.

One measure of intimacy with someone is the degree to which we can be honest with him or her. Jeremiah knows God so well that he knows he can speak to His face without being destroyed by lightning. His raw words lead through repentance and praise but just when we think Jeremiah has found his faith once again, we hear this in Jeremiah 20:14: "Cursed be the day I was born!"

What comes next? Nothing. That's right. No apology

from God and no apology from Jeremiah. The Holy Spirit chooses to cover in silence whatever conversation they had next. We don't know what God did or what Jeremiah did.

We do know that Jeremiah was still alive and still prophesying, and God was still caring for him and using him. Listen to God's Word spoken to and through Jeremiah in 29:11: "'I know the plans I have for you,' declares the LORD, 'plans to prosper you and not to harm you, plans to give you hope and a future.'"

And God shows the relationship between intimacy and honesty, between seeking Him and crying out to Him in our pain: "'Then you will call upon me and come and pray to me, and I will listen to you. You will seek me and find me when you seek me with all your heart. I will be found by you,' declares the LORD" (Jeremiah 29:12–14).

What is the point? We seek God as we are, not as we should be. We ask Him real, not hypothetical, questions. And God is found, even when we are lonely, doubting, or mad as, well, you know.

But what do we do when our seeking leads to silence, when we see contradictions between what we read in the Bible and what we see in the world? When I read something confusing or apparently contradictory in the Bible, I don't assume the apparent contradiction suggests God is unfaithful. I try to assume that my confusion reveals how much I have yet to grow in my own understanding of the mystery of God.

Having said this, I am struck by how difficult this is to do in the rough and tumble of life in the dark. If God promises peace and I'm in turmoil, what do I do? If God offers me relationship with Him, why do I still feel alone? It's to this mystery that we turn next.

◊ ◊ ◊

Look at the lonely life of Christ for a model of our hide-and-seek relationship with the Father.

Jesus received word that John had been beheaded: "When Jesus heard what had happened, he withdrew by boat privately to a solitary place" (Matthew 14:13).

Why?

Jesus was grieving over the loss of a friend. The people find out where Jesus is going and they walk to meet him. His private grief is interrupted, but he feels compassion for the people. He feeds them—all five thousand of them—miraculously. Afterward Jesus sends His disciples away by boat and He goes off to pray by Himself again.

When He sees His disciples in trouble on the sea, He walks toward them on the water. They see Him, think He is a ghost, and are terrified. "But Jesus immediately said to them: 'Take courage! It is I. Don't be afraid' (Matthew 14:27).

The wind stopped, and the disciples were completely amazed, "For they had not understood about the loaves; their hearts were hardened" (Mark 6:52).

Jesus had been praying, probably in part because He knew His disciples still had hard hearts. *What do I need to do to help them believe, Father? I just fed five thousand people with a few fish and five loaves of bread.* But mostly He wanted to be with God.

Later, Jesus is confronted by Pharisees and teachers of the law over issues of ceremonial washing: "You hypocrites! Isaiah was right when he prophesied about you: 'These people honor me with their lips, but their hearts are far from me'" (Matthew 15:7–8).

Afterward His disciples came to Him in private to ask Him what he meant (see Matthew 15:12). Jesus sees their hearts. *Are you so dull? Don't you see?*

He feeds another crowd of people, some four thousand, and again His disciples don't understand or believe. Immediately afterward they are on a boat with only one loaf of bread. (They forgot to bring more, when they had seven baskets full at their feet!)

Do you still not understand? Are your hearts hardened?

Do you have eyes but fail to see, and ears but fail to hear? And don't you remember?

Do you still not understand?

And then Peter makes his wonderful confession—"You are the Christ" (Matthew 16:16)—followed by his arrogant rebuke of Jesus.

Jesus saw how Peter's statement affected the rest of the disciples. He rebuked Peter: "Get behind me, Satan! . . . you do not have in mind the things of God, but the things of men" (Matthew 16:23).

Should Jesus be feeling alone yet?

Six days later Jesus takes Peter, James, and John and goes up on the mountain to pray. All that we have studied in the life of Christ prepares us for what happens next.

The Father has heard the prayers of His Son. He has watched the loneliness of Jesus. He has seen enough! *And God the Father moves heaven and earth to be found by His Son, and to care for His Son.*

He calls to Moses, "Now you may go into the 'promised land.' But this isn't for you; it's for My Son. Elijah, you, too, will go." And the Father cuts through the fabric that separates the spiritual from the physical, dispatching these heroes of the faith to be with Jesus.

Why these two? Why not two others?

Moses had led Israel; he knew better than any other

person their proud hearts. He also knew the loneliness of God's call. He is the one whose face was transfigured by the glory of God, but that very glory set him even more apart from his people.

And Elijah. He watched God destroy the priests of Baal. Then he ran into the desert and cried, "I have had enough, LORD" (1 Kings 19:4). And later in the cave, "I am the only one left" (1 Kings 19:10).

God cared so much for His Son that He sent these two men back to earth to comfort and encourage Jesus.

This was not for the disciples.

This was for Jesus.

Luke tells us, "They spoke about his departure, which he was about to bring to fulfillment at Jerusalem" (Luke 9:31). They reminded Jesus that He was close to accomplishing His purpose. They reminded Him that He was coming back home to heaven.

Jesus stands there transfigured by the presence of the glory of God the Father. (He had left His own glory behind when He came to earth.) The mount of transfiguration was about *how far a Father will go to meet the needs of His Son.*

Jesus was the loneliest person to walk the face of the earth. He left a perfect heaven and an eternal face-to-face presence with His Father—where the Three in One was never lonely—to come to a cursed world where He could be surrounded by people and yet still feel abandoned. And at the end He cried, "My God, my God, why have you forsaken me?" (Mark 15:34). A most profound loneliness. But the end was the beginning.

Only the lonely seek God.

Jesus was the loneliest person to walk the face of the earth.

Jesus sought God the Father more than any one ever has. Sometimes we are lonely for all the right reasons.

It's okay for us to admit it. It's not heaven yet. And it's dark in here. And those voices . . .

We forgot something in the first blush of having all of our sins forgiven. Forgiven people can be lonely. There is no shame in this. This hide-and-seek is no game God teases us with. It is about God pursuing lonely children with the love of a Father. And children responding in faith as they pursue a God who wants to be found.

"How great is the love the Father has lavished on us, that we should be called children of God! And that is what we are!" (1 John 3:1). God our Father will move heaven and earth to be found by His children.

◊ ◊ ◊

God invites lonely sons and daughters to seek and find Him. The One cared so much about so many, that He made them weak. . . .

the giver
of weakness

*"Never anxious.
Never surprised,
yet never bored,
that alone must
be some kind
of definition
of deity."*

It is a paradox. We were perfectly designed to be imperfect. We were made *imago Dei*, "in the image of God," yet we have weakness.

And the astute student will reply, "Huh? Weren't we created holy, without sin? Then Eve and Adam stepped away from God and His strength and into sin and weakness. But we weren't *created* to be weak."

That's true, but it's not all the truth. God created Adam and Eve with needs before they fell into sin.

We naturally think of weakness and sin as synonymous, but it "ain't necessarily so" (with apologies to Ira Gershwin). Adam and Eve needed oxygen to breathe, food to eat, earth to walk on, sun to keep warm, fresh water to drink, gravity to hold the place together. And after God made all necessary infrastructure for survival He said, "It is good."

Not only was the supply for our need "good," it was created before our needs existed. The fish were not left floundering on the ground until the oceans and lakes were created. The water came first and then the fish.

Every need you and I have came after God made the provision for the need. *This means that my daily needs are a daily reminder of God's provision, ready to be received by faith.* Of course, this is easy to write until I get a bill in the mail telling me my house payment is due. . . .

This must be true because of the nature of our God. Every provision we need comes from who He is. When we ask, God doesn't need to scramble to find an answer. He is the answer. He was the answer before the question was asked.

So as natural as it is for you and me to have needs, it is natural for God to meet needs. As natural as it is for us to be weak, it is natural for God to be strong. It's a part of who we are, and it is who God is.

Why did God do it this way? He could easily have made us needing nothing. We could never be hungry for food or gasping for air. No thirst for water. But God made us weak so we would turn to Him and in our turning glorify Him. Our weaknesses remind us again of who He is and who we are, of how we are called to further *His* reputation because of His loving provision for us.

God does not offer an apology for how He created us, though we often stand there tapping our foot, hands on our hips, waiting for one. This, too, is an apology that will never come.

◊ ◊ ◊

Let's consider the story of a member of God's "honor roll of faith" in Hebrews chapter 11. Say hello to an unlikely hero, Gideon.

We find Gideon's story beginning in the sixth chapter of

Judges. The book of Judges is more than a history of Israel's failure to trust God. It is a record of God's grace to a rebellious people. The cyclical narratives reveal how much the Father pursues and wants to be pursued by His children.

After Joshua and his elders died, "another generation grew up, who knew neither the LORD nor what he had done for Israel. . . . They forsook the LORD. . . . They followed and worshiped various gods of the peoples around them" (Judges 2:10, 12).

Israel's people rejected God so God gave them over to their enemies. After eight years of slavery, they cried out to God for mercy. He sent a judge named Othniel to rescue them. They had forty years of peace until their judge died. Then they forgot God again and served other gods, and God punished them . . . and the cycle continued.

Our story picks up after Israel has been subject to the Midianites for eight years. So many of these nomads descended on Israel's land and ravaged crops that they were described as "locusts" (Judges 7:12).

God hears the cry of His people and one day an angel surprises a man.

Gideon was hiding out in the mountains, grinding grain in a winepress. The Midianites would never think to look in a winepress for food, since it wasn't the season for grapes yet. This was the hard way to grind grain, but better than losing the crop altogether to this hated enemy.

Judges chapter 6 says, "The angel of the LORD came and sat down under the oak" (v. 11). Apparently he watched Gideon for a while before he made his presence known to him. And the angel must have had a slight smile on his face when he surprised Gideon: "The LORD is with you, mighty warrior" (v. 12).

God calls this timid man hiding behind a winepress, "mighty warrior." Gideon doesn't think it's too funny. Perhaps without stopping his work, and maybe barely even acknowledging his guest, Gideon replies, "If the LORD is with us, why has all this happened to us?" He gestures to the winepress and wipes the sweat off his forehead. "Where are all his wonders [and we might hear sarcasm as he whines 'wonders'] that our fathers told us about? . . . But now the LORD has abandoned us and put us into the hand of Midian" (v. 13).

And the angel, now called "the LORD" (v. 14), turns to him. (This is what theologians refer to as a *theophany*. The appearance of the Lord in a physical form as though He is an angel. You see, it is the Lord pursuing Gideon.)

"Go in the strength you have and save Israel out of Midian's hand. Am I not sending you?" (v. 14).

But again Gideon (the mighty warrior), protests, "But Lord . . . how can I save Israel? My clan is the weakest in Manasseh, and [if that's not enough] I am the least in my family" (v. 15).

God doesn't say, "O Gideon, don't be so hard on yourself." Instead, His silence confirms, *Yes, you really are that weak, Gideon, I agree—you are the least in your family! But I've chosen you nevertheless.*

God prophesies, "I will be with you, and you will strike down all the Midianites together" (v. 16).

All? The people so numerous that they are described as locusts? Now comes the first of a series of signs.

Gideon asks the Lord to wait while he kills a goat and prepares an offering. *If He is who He says He is, He'll wait.*

The Lord says "I will wait until you return" (v. 18).

How long does it take a "mighty warrior" to catch a

goat, kill it, cook it, make bread, and prepare the offering? Gideon isn't sure anybody would wait that long, but if he does, then maybe he is sincere.

When he comes back out, the Lord is waiting. That's the first sign. But now Gideon is given more signs. The angel of God tells Gideon to put all the food on a rock, which he does. Then the angel touches the sacrifice with his staff, and fire comes shooting out from the rock and consumes the meat and bread.

"And the angel of the LORD disappeared" (v. 21).

A moment ago fire shot out from a rock, and now the angel who was standing there vanishes from sight.

And Gideon, the "mighty warrior" falls down on his face. God sees his terrified heart and hears his cry.

"Ah, Sovereign LORD! I have seen the angel of the LORD face to face!" (v. 22).

God gives him yet another sign. An invisible voice begins speaking to Gideon.

"Peace! Do not be afraid. You are not going to die" (v. 23).

God knows what we need to hear.

So Gideon worships God there.

When we see the One as He is, we see ourselves as we are. Our "reputation" that we have cultivated so long seems frail and worthless. We are terrified and humbled; the only response we have is to worship.

Later that same night (it's been a big day for the "mighty warrior"), God again speaks to Gideon and tells him to destroy his father's idols. Gideon is afraid, so he waits until the middle of the night to do it. But he obeys God.

Are we getting used to the idea that Gideon is not so brave and strong? God speaks to him anyway, and Gideon listens.

Now, if the Midianites were not fearful enough, the Amalekites and "other eastern peoples joined forces" (v. 33). So "the Spirit of the LORD came upon Gideon" (v. 34) and he gathers the army of Israel together, some 32,000 men.

But Gideon is still afraid and asks God for another sign. He tells God, "'Look, I will place a wool fleece on the threshing floor. If there is dew only on the fleece and all the ground is dry, then I will know that you will save Israel by my hand'" (vv. 36–37).

And God does it.

But then Gideon asks God, "Do not be angry with me. Let me make just one more request" (v. 39). In case it was just a coincidence. In case it was just "luck," do it again but reverse it—let the wool fleece be dry and the ground wet. And God does it for him.

Now if we were God, what would we do with Gideon and his requests? Probably we'd take it personally, assume Gideon didn't trust us, never had, and replace him with someone easier to work with.

We've heard the sermons blasting Gideon for his unbelief. But what if Gideon believes God more than we realize?

Consider this example. We read in the first chapter of Luke about another man, a priest by the name of Zechariah, who is visited by an angel. The angel tells him that his prayers have been answered.

"Which prayers are those?" He and his wife, Elizabeth, have been unable to have children. They prayed about it for years but stopped praying about it when they got so old. Now they are going to have a baby. This would be good news to most couples but this priest is about a hundred years old, and so is his wife. That's a little late to be starting a family. He asks the angel for a sign.

Now does this sound vaguely familiar? Sounds like Gideon, doesn't it?

Angels.

Frightened men.

Promises that seem too good to be true.

The request for signs.

Sounds like Zechariah must have been reading his Old Testament lesson, "What to Do If Visited by Angels."

But when Zechariah asks for a sign, the angel rebukes him: "I am Gabriel. I stand in the presence of God, and I have been sent to speak to you and to tell you this good news. And now you will be silent and not able to speak until the day this happens, *because you did not believe* my words, which will come true at their proper time" (Luke 1:19–20).

God knows the difference between hearts. He knew Gideon's heart and gave him each sign with no rebuke.

Is it possible Gideon is saying, "Give me these signs because I don't trust my ability to recognize Your will? I want to do Your will, and I need to be sure this is it. It's not that I think You are not trustworthy, Lord—I'm just not sure about myself."

And the signs aren't over yet.

Early the next morning, God speaks to Gideon again. "I have a problem with the number of men you have, Gideon."

"Me too! I was hoping You'd notice how few I've got, Lord. How could I defeat an army of about 135,000 with my little band of 32,000? Thanks for hearing my prayers."

"No, Gideon, that's not what I mean."

"It's not?"

"No, I think you have too many soldiers!"

"Too many?"

"When you conquer the Midianites and their allies, the nations will think you did it by your own power and you will receive glory that belongs to Me. So Gideon, tell everyone who is afraid that they can go home" (see Judges 7:1–3).

If I were God and wanted to keep Gideon as my general over the troops, I'd never tell him this. I'd be afraid he would be the first to leave and go home!

Gideon makes the announcement and probably closes his eyes, afraid to see who and how many are running away.

When he opens his eyes, only 10,000 men are left. Two-thirds of the men went home (see 7:3).

God again speaks to him and says, "There are still too many men" (7:4).

Hundreds of sermons have been preached on why God uses such a strange way to reduce the numbers: "Separate those who lap the water with their tongues like a dog from those who kneel down to drink" (7:5). The sermons explain that one group of men will be better soldiers than the other group because those soldiers are always ready to stand and fight. Maybe.

But if God wanted the best soldiers, why did he start with Gideon? If God wants the best soldiers, why does He take away their weapons and give them trumpets and torches?

Maybe God is simply reducing the numbers so that it will be apparent to all that He is God and we are not.

We come now to the night before the battle.

Listen to the kindness of our God. See the grace of God: "Gideon, are you afraid?"

"O yes, Lord, you know I'm afraid."

God doesn't scold him for being afraid. Instead he does

what a loving Father would do—He extends grace and mercy. How does He do it? Oh listen, this is great stuff!

"Gideon, do you want another sign?"

Who said Gideon needed signs because he didn't believe? Maybe he was just human, like you and me. *God, give us signs today. We still need them; we're still human!*

Of course Gideon said yes. So God told him to take his servant and go down to the tents of Midian and listen to a conversation. Why the servant too? Well, if Gideon has trouble believing his own ears, maybe it will help if he has another set of ears along. And one more witness could be helpful when encouraging his men to go to battle.

Gideon and the servant hear one Midianite soldier share his dream with the other: "I saw a loaf of bread roll down a hill and wipe out a Midianite tent that was standing there." The second man confirms that this dream indeed promises victory to Gideon.

And Gideon, who recognizes the faithfulness of his God, worships Him right there outside the tents of Midian (see 7:9–15).

But the fight is yet to be fought and Gideon returns to prepare his men for the battle. "Dividing the three hundred men into three companies, he placed trumpets and empty jars into the hands of all of them, with torches inside" (7:16).

And one of the men turns to another and says, "Did I miss something? When were the auditions held? I don't know how to play this thing." Another says, "I knew I should have written one last note to my wife to tell her I love her."

Gideon ignores the looks of dismay and continues. "Follow my lead. . . . When I and all who are with me blow our trumpets, then from around the camp, [by the way, how

do three hundred men surround a camp of 135,000?] blow
your trumpets, and shout, 'For the LORD and for Gideon'"
(7:17–18).

A man turns to his buddy. "What, are we nuts? The darkness, I like that. But if I'm holding up a torch, their archers
know where to shoot their arrows. I've given them a perfect
target, but I still can't see them to fight back."

Why did God tell Gideon to do something so foolish?
God took the weapons out of Israel's hands so they had no
chance to claim the glory. See why the quality of fighter in
Gideon's army was a moot point? Perhaps God told them to
hold up the torches not as much as a strategy of surprise to
confuse the enemy, but as a light in a dark world. God
wanted them to see His victory. God wanted them to be
witnesses to His saving power. *He wanted them to see God
doing what only God can do.*

And God caused confusion in the camp, and the
Midianites began killing one another in the confusion (see
7:22). Gideon and his three hundred men watched as God
received all the glory for His victory.

Isn't this a wonderful picture of evangelism? We hold up
the light and watch God do what only God can do. We
don't save anybody; it's God's doing. It's not to our glory
when another prisoner of the dark believes in Jesus; it is the
Holy Spirit working.

Do you see God's strategy from the beginning? He
chose a weak man, loved him, laughed at him (we take
ourselves way too seriously!), and used him.

"I can do all things through him who strengthens me"
(Philippians 4:13 ESV). This means that I need something—I
need strength.

This also means that God could design me in my

mother's womb, in spite of my parents' sin in my conception, and use a weak, painfully insecure man who seems
to be constantly trying to justify himself to others. God
convicts, forgives, sanctifies, and while all of that is going
on (not just after it's complete), He uses me.

◊ ◊ ◊

Designed perfectly imperfect. Praise God!
Now we can stop performing and learn to laugh,
learn to let God do what only God can do,
for His glory alone. . . .

the giver
of grace

*"Every true prayer
that's ever been
prayed, every
longing to embrace
all that's good and
right, and every love
inspired by faith
is a gift of grace."*

L ife is tough and then you die." That summarizes the worldview of most people, including many Christians. But maybe there is another way to see the world: "Life is tough, but God is good." That was how one of my seminary profs summarized the book of Psalms. Psalm 130 begins, "Out of the depths I cry to you" (Psalm 130:1). *Don't I seem to spend a lot of time down here, Lord, in the "depths"?*

In John 16, Jesus gives us a promise that none of us wants to claim. He said, "In this world you will have trouble." But I often forget the rest of it: "Take heart! I have overcome the world" (John 16:33).

We do have trouble in this world. I need God's grace to help me through the hardness of life. I hurt people with my words, and I am sometimes hurt by others. Some days every traffic light is red and the rain seems to be pouring just on me. First Peter chapter 5 reminded me one day years ago that God gives grace, and if I want it, He is the one I have to go to in order to find it.

But I also discovered that He doesn't just throw it out there for anybody. God gives grace to a certain kind of person. Peter says God opposes the proud but gives grace to the humble (see 1 Peter 5:5).

And I realized I had a problem.

Humility had never been one of those qualities that I admired most about myself. I could only imagine what kind of a weak performer I might be if I were profoundly humble. I worked hard trying to build my reputation and I thought humility would destroy all my hard work. But here was my dilemma—there were only two choices. God opposes the proud but gives grace to the humble. It was either pride or humility.

The topic of my master's thesis in seminary was the spiritual needs of Christian musicians, both professionals and amateurs. After surveying hundreds of musicians and asking them, "What are your greatest spiritual needs?" I found that one of the top three needs was this: "How can I be professional without being proud?"

I proceeded to throw Bible verses at the problem as if I were throwing pies up against a wall to see which ones would stick. I traveled and spoke on the subject but truthfully I had no answer strong enough to change my own proud heart.

As I read further in Peter's letter, I realized why not. I was being opposed by God because of my stubborn heart.

We think *humility* means being a doormat that people can step on when they walk into a room. We imagine *humility* means always taking the back row or the back seat. Humility feels to us—well, I'll tell you what it feels like. In the Broadway musical *Camelot*, there's a scene where King Arthur's illegitimate nephew Mordred is mocking the virtues of life. This is what he says about humility: "Humility means to be hurt. It's not the earth the meek inherit, it's the dirt."

Humility's been given a bad name and most of us have believed it. But in order to understand humility, let's look at pride first.

◊ ◊ ◊

Imagine pride wearing two faces. The first, and the most obvious, face is that sneering look of disdain from arrogant eyes. It's that politician who's looking down at you or that rock star or star athlete who knows he is better than you. It's the look that makes you feel worthless. We've all felt it and we all hate it. That's the look Solomon talks about in Proverbs—the "haughty eyes" (21:4). But pride has another face and this face is a surprise to us.

This is the face of self-pity. These are the eyes that look at you or me and say, "Nobody understands me, nobody likes me or cares about me." But you see, the focus of self-pity is the same as the focus of the arrogant eyes. It's about me. *What do people think about me?* And you and I have seen this look of self-pity in the church. You might call this group the professional weaker brothers and sisters:

"You wouldn't want to come between *me* and Jesus with the kind of music you're listening to, would you?"

"The way that you wear your chartreuse hair causes *me* to stumble."

"It really hurts *me* that you don't try to understand me."

"I feel like nobody cares about *me* and my opinion."

"I'm a sensitive person, and you need to be extra careful in dealing with *me*."

You see, self-pity puts the focus on the same place that the arrogant eyes do—not on others, on us.

I was explaining this to a friend recently, and he inter-rupted me: "Paul, I'm guilty of both faces! Whichever one I need to wear in order to get what I want."

Right! Me too!

I've seen in myself the capability of going either direc-tion with pride, whichever is most effective for the moment.

Whatever face pride wears, its intent is to try to control others and manipulate their thoughts about us. If I can't get you to do what I want you to do by some arrogant look of intimidation, then I'll try to get you to do what I want you to do by making you feel sorry for me. *I'm a very sensitive person.* . . . Both strategies come from pride. Both are after control. And God is opposed to both.

◊ ◊ ◊

For a great example of pride, look in Luke's Gospel, chapter 14. Jesus tells this story when He notices how His disciples were choosing the places of honor. He tells them that if they are not careful, they would be like a man who comes into a banquet hall and as he walks in the door he pauses and surveys the room. His eyes stop when he locates the head table. Very deliberately—so that no one will miss it—he strides to the front of the room and chooses a place at the head table.

He realizes that all eyes are on him as he enters. That was his goal. He's a performer. His reputation is everything to him. He's sitting there and he picks up a glass of wine and begins to sip it with great pomp and circumstance. How do you drink a glass of wine with pomp and circum-stance? Well, he's practiced and he's good.

While he's sipping his wine and looking at the peasants looking at him, he senses some motion behind him. Maybe he feels an arm brush up against him, maybe he hears a voice. Then someone addresses him: "Friend, I don't know how to tell you this, but the place that you are sitting in was reserved for someone else. In fact, all of the places at this head table are reserved for others. But I'm certain that you will find a comfortable seat out there at the back of our banquet hall. Thank you for being so understanding."

Now this man who came in so arrogantly has to figure out how he's going to get from this place at the head table all the way to the back of the room without anyone noticing him. He stands up irritated and embarrassed. Maybe his face is already turning red. His lips have tightened. And as he makes his way to the back, all eyes are on him. Because God is opposed to the proud but gives grace to the humble.

This man found himself face to face with God and God won. God will always win. He is the One, the One and Only. We are only the many. You can bet that as that man walks to the back of the hall, he doesn't look for another seat. He walks as fast as his legs will carry him, trying not to make eye contact with anyone, although he notices a couple chuckling at him. He goes out the back door, muttering curses as he leaves.

◊ ◊ ◊

At the beginning of this chapter, I said I understood that life is tough and I want God's grace, but as I read Peter I realize what my choices are. If I want God's grace, I must be the kind of person He gives grace to—humble. But it is a struggle.

The intensity of my struggle struck me again several years ago when my wife and I were training to join the staff of World Harvest Mission. Each week, my wife and I faxed homework to a mentor and then called our mentor from our home in Nashville to discuss the topic of that week's assignment.

I often wondered if Richard, our mentor, thought there was only one person on the phone—me. He would say, "Paul, you have a real problem with your anger, don't you?" I was mad because he pointed it out with my wife listening, only confirming what all of us knew. And maybe the next week he'd say, "I can see you're sure struggling with some issues of truthfulness." I'd say that I wanted to be a trustworthy man. And we'd talk about it. Did I mention that I need a Savior?

Well, this particular week the topic had been pride. We were asked to choose from a list of "surface sins"—such as lying, gluttony, laziness, swearing, and lusting—and write about how pride affected that sin in our lives.

Now, keep in mind that our mentor was going to read whatever I wrote and we were going to talk about it with my wife on the phone too. Being the performer that I am, desperate to build and preserve my reputation, I decided that I needed to find—somewhere in this long list of potential surface sins—a safe sin.

You know what I mean by "safe" don't you? I needed to find a sin that my mentor and my wife would nod their heads at and say, "Yeah, that's a problem for me too." Or maybe they would yawn and promptly forget what it was. I wanted to find a sin that was vanilla, not memorable like Moose Tracks or Rocky Road. The performer in me was on full alert.

So I looked down this list and thought, *Now let's see, I can't say* deceitfulness *because then he's going to wonder how much I've lied about before now. I probably don't want to say* anger *because we've already been down that road and maybe he's going to want to know, "Just how angry does he get? Is he dangerous; does he throw things?"* Oh, of course I don't want to say lust *because there's nothing that travels faster on a prayer request line than an announcement that you have moral problems.*

So, I searched the list and I found it: the perfect sin. It was exactly what I wanted—one of those sins that no one would notice, everyone would confess, and everyone would forget.

Do you want to know what it was?

It was the sin of an undisciplined heart.

Isn't that great?

An undisciplined heart . . . who cares? Who notices? Nobody's going to call and say, "Pray for Paul. He's got an undisciplined heart, poor guy."

So I sat down and began to write—and quickly discovered that this sin wasn't nearly as safe as I had hoped it to be. Pride affected my undisciplined heart with my first words.

I wrote:

> *I am intuitive and creative so I can think better on my feet than others. I don't need to prepare ahead of time. I'm smart enough to wing it where others who are less intelligent must plan their thoughts ahead of time.*

Sounds pretty bad, doesn't it? It gets worse.

> *The artist, the musician in me doesn't want to be restricted by hard and fast rules. Don't limit me with tracks to run on. Tracks are great for a train, but they*

can be so boring. Personally I prefer the adventure that being completely out of control brings. Discipline is for those who are dull, less creative. A lack of discipline is freeing.

But God was there, and that's good, not bad, and I heard Him.

The truth is my undisciplined heart is waging war with the disciplined heart of God for control of my life. To defend a lack of discipline is to argue for my right to rule as I please. I want to be the exception. If there's a sign on the door that says "Private, No Admittance," I want to open the door and ask why. If there's a sign that says "No Parking Here," I want to park there and ask who says I can't.

I find rules to be confining. But God's design of my personality and His gifting is meant to function best within the limits of the gospel. My heart is evil. My intuition is a poor substitute for the leading of the Holy Spirit.

Well, my mentor read these things and said, "Paul, do you want me to tell you what your problem is?"

I promise you that nothing in me wanted to hear what he had to say next. I wanted to say, "There's somebody else on the line here. Why don't you talk to my wife? She's got issues too."

The mentor said, "I'll tell you what the problem is. Your problem, Paul, is that you want to have the right to rule. The right to control life around you. You want to be God."

I hated hearing it, but I couldn't forget it. I had a hard time sleeping that night as I thought about the ramifications. What does it mean that I am competing with the God of the universe for the right to rule? And I prayed, "God, make me humble. I mean, if You give grace and You only give it to a humble person, make me humble."

The only thing more dangerous than asking for humility is not asking!

◊ ◊ ◊

As I began to think more about what it meant to be humble, God pointed me toward the person of Jesus. Paul writes in the second chapter of Philippians that Jesus humbled himself by becoming obedient. Even to the point of death on a cross. I remember the day this stopped me in my tracks as I was studying this chapter. How did Jesus become humble? By becoming obedient.

All of this time I'd been praying that God would make me humble. But humility comes from obedience. Not simply a list of rules—do this, do that, and do this—but a heart submitted to the Father. First Peter chapter 5 came to my mind. When I looked there, I saw something I had missed before. God shows us what obedience looks like. He shows us what humility looks like. He says, "Humble yourselves, therefore, under the mighty hand of God so that at the proper time He may exalt you, casting all your anxieties on him because he cares for you" (vv. 6–7 ESV).

That's obedience.

Obedience is letting God be God. This was what I had missed those years I was traveling around telling people how to be humble. Obedience is letting God do what only God can do. It's holding up the torches with Gideon in order to see God fighting the battle.

I thought obedience was going to be, Did I have my quiet time, did I pray last night, did I share Christ with my neighbor? It's much more profound than that. And it's much lighter than that.

Do you remember what Jesus said in Matthew 11? "Come to me, all you who are weary and burdened, and I will give you rest. Take my yoke upon you. . . . For my yoke is easy and my burden is light" (vv. 28–30). Most of us have imagined that obedience is a heavy burden we carry. That's what the law feels like. But to begin to understand the grace of God is to exchange our heavy burdens for the light burden of Christ. John agrees: "This is love for God: to obey his commands. And his commands are not burdensome, for everyone born of God overcomes the world. This is the victory that has overcome the world, even our faith" (1 John 5:3–4).

We have here a beautiful picture of the "lightness" of love. Obedience means casting onto Jesus the things that are weighing my heart down. Good things as well as bad things. The pain in my heart over a friend who's not repenting. The confusion in my heart over a decision difficult to make. The frustration of potential not realized. Or for a performer like me, success not recognized. Casting all my cares on Him. That's obedience. That's part of what it means to love God with all I am.

And that's the mark of humility. Because proud people won't cast their cares on God. They say to themselves, *I can do it. I can fix this. Give me a little bit more time; I can make it right.* Those aren't noble intentions. Those are marks of a proud heart. So I said, "Jesus, I want grace and grace is given to a humble person. So make me humble. I know that

You humbled Yourself by becoming obedient, so I want to be obedient too."

Then one day I discovered another passage. I think it was another one of those verses God dropped into the Bible overnight while I was sleeping: "Jesus offered up prayers and supplications, with loud cries and tears, to him who was able to save him from death, and he was heard *because of his reverence*" (Hebrews 5:7 ESV). Jesus honored God by revering Him, which is to obey Him from the heart. He cast His cares on God as an act of reverence, an act of obedience.

But it's the last part of the next verse that shook me to my roots. "He learned obedience through what he suffered" (Hebrews 5:8 ESV). I shuddered as I began to grasp this truth. *If it took suffering to teach Jesus obedience, what will it take to teach me to obey? If the Son of Man had to suffer to learn obedience, how do I imagine I can escape suffering and still learn to obey God?*

We may want to be obedient, but we rarely seek out suffering. I think of the time a friend of ours went to the store to buy flour our first year in Ukraine. She tried out her limited Russian vocabulary: "May I have a kilogram of *moocah*?" The woman behind the counter laughed and replied, "You can have some of mine!" The other women joined in behind the counter, "Mine too!" "Here, take it all!" another called out, and more laughter.

Our friend was puzzled by the response and after returning home she called her interpreter friend and asked what that was about.

Her translator laughed when she heard the story and then explained.

"There are two words that sound similar: *mucaah* and *moocah*. The first is the word for *flour*. The word you used is the second one. That word is our Russian word for *suffering!*"

Our friend had been asking for a kilogram of suffering. No wonder the women were so willing to give their *moocah* to her!

Sometimes we don't always know what we are asking God for. I can almost hear God saying, "Paul, make up your mind. You tell me You want to be like Jesus, and then you tell Me to take away your suffering. What do you want?" And of course my junior high answer is to say, "I want to be like Jesus and I don't want to suffer."

But at the same moment, I begin to see God has been faithful to me all along. He has been there in the middle of my suffering. Growing my heart, patiently bringing me to this place where I can say with an honest heart I still want to be like Jesus, whatever that means.

◊ ◊ ◊

It was six o'clock in the morning in Kiev when the telephone rang. It was my brother Bruce calling from the States to tell me of the death of my father. My father, the alcoholic, had given his heart to Jesus during my last year of high school and been set free from his addiction to drinking. We had prayed together, sung hymns at the rescue mission together, and shared food and faith with prisoners in the jails. In his last phone call to me, he had told me once again how proud he was of me. And now he was gone. I was in shock. I paced around the apartment, my mind spinning as I tried to take it all in.

My wife encouraged me to come back to bed and pray together about this. I didn't want to, but I went back to bed anyway. My body shook as I sobbed. I could hardly breathe. It was the worst day of my life, the worst hour of my life. I cried out to God in my sobbing but had to pause periodically just to catch my breath.

In those brief pauses, I felt as though God somehow left His throne and came directly to me. I've never known anything like it before or since. But with each breath, God came to me, as one Father understanding how deeply I ached over the loss of another father. In those moments of my greatest suffering, God was most real. And I knew something of the grace of God in His presence as I cast my deepest cares on Him.

In the midst of my grief, I didn't set out to follow a formula of obedience. Only looking back could I see how my experience reflected the pattern of grace I was discovering: Life is tough; we need grace. God gives grace to the humble. Jesus humbled Himself by becoming obedient. Obedience means to revere God as God. I cast my cares on Him. I stop pretending to be God.

And the most difficult thing to discover: Jesus learned obedience through what He suffered. When I receive suffering as God's gift, suffering becomes God's way—in addition to His Word—to make me like Christ. It is one of God's "means of grace" in my life.

As I become more like Christ through the grace of God—and through the suffering of Christ—I don't care as much about building myself up. The giver of grace allows me to let go of my compulsion to develop my own reputation and invites me to discover more of His.

◊ ◊ ◊

It was a short flight home from the mountains of San Luis Obispo, California, to the smog of San Bernardino. Short, but unforgettable. . . .

*"Integrity,
a reflection
in His eyes,
the bluest sky
shining in
the clearest
pond."*

CHAPTER 14

vertigo

I was asked to do a concert at a conference in the beautiful mountains of San Luis Obispo, in northern California.

It was an unusual opportunity. The concert organizers asked a friend of theirs, a private pilot, to pick me up from my home in southern California. I took my son Jonathan with me. It was going to be a nice father-son adventure.

And that it was.

The day before the concert, the pilot picked us up near our home in San Bernardino and we headed north. We checked into a hotel near the airport. After set-up and a sound check, Jon and I went back to our hotel to clean up and then returned for the concert.

When we woke up the next morning we looked out the window at intense grey. We couldn't see a thing; it was as thick a fog as I've ever experienced.

The phone rang. It was the pilot asking us if we were ready to go home.

I looked out the window and asked him if the weather was a problem. (I imagined that pilots like to see where they're going.) He said we would be safe; he could fly on "instrument panels" for our takeoff and once we broke through the clouds we'd have blue sky and "visual" the remainder of the flight.

I agreed and we arranged to meet after breakfast.

Driving to the airport, I again mentioned my concern about the heavy fog, and the pilot again laughed and said not to worry; everything would be fine.

We taxied down the runway in our little Piper Cub plane and lifted off. Our beginning ascent seemed steep, but recalling that we were surrounded by mountains, I figured that was a good idea.

Suddenly the plane began to rock from side to side. I looked at the pilot and saw his face was pure white. Then the bottom seemed to drop from under us and it felt as if we were plunging downward. I blurted out, "Praise the Lord!"

Looking back on it, I guess I could have said a lot worse given the circumstances. The pilot responded without taking his eyes off the instrument panel in front of him, "Amen!"

Now I don't know what you think of when you hear "Amen," but I could've suggested more hopeful responses. When I hear "Amen" I think of *endings*, not beginnings! I'm not sure if he even heard himself in those moments.

Then just as suddenly as everything had gone crazy, the plane seemed to level out and resume its ascent. In seconds we burst through the clouds. That bright sun never looked more inviting!

The pilot turned to me as exhausted as he was relieved and said, "Vertigo almost got us."

I must have looked puzzled, which of course I was, and

he explained.

"*Vertigo* is the name given to the body's response when the fluid inside the inner ear is set in motion. It's like what happens when someone blindfolds you and has you sit on a piano stool and spins you around and around, and then asks you to point to some object in the room, which you are unable to see, and of course you can't do it. Vertigo gives you a false sense of reality, and if a pilot suffers from this and trusts his feelings, he will think he is going up when he is really going down, or going left when he is going right."

He said somberly, "Vertigo kills a lot of pilots."

"What do they do to overcome such strong feelings?" I asked.

"They have to trust the instrument panel in front of them. They have to have something more objective than their emotions to trust in."

And I thought to myself, *What a powerful illustration of the Christian life.*

How many of us have plowed into the side of a mountain somewhere emotionally because we were overcome by "vertigo"? We needed objective truth to interpret those haunting voices.

◊ ◊ ◊

As a musician, I've sat in front of an audience and felt the "electricity" in the air and been energized to give a strong concert.

I've had other experiences too. Early in my performing career I was backstage in Dallas, preparing to come out for a concert. The guy who set it up was enthusiastic but very young and inexperienced. He had put up fliers in various places advertising the concert, but that was all he did.

When I was introduced, I walked out onto a beautiful stage with a new nine-foot Steinway grand piano next to my electric keyboard, facing a twelve-hundred-seat auditorium. You could smell the plush, heavy, new velvet curtains.

I was welcomed by the thunderous applause of about fifteen people! I sat at the piano stunned. I said to myself, *I'm a professional. I don't have to do this concert. I could just walk back out rather than suffer the humiliation of performing for a handful of people.* But I sensed God saying, "Do this concert for Me."

Nothing inside me felt like continuing, but I did. And as much as possible I tried to give myself to God and to each song as if the auditorium were packed full. I was still young myself and I'm sure it wasn't perfect, but my heart was right before God and I was learning more important lessons about humility.

We musicians and artists tend to live by our feelings in part because that's how God has wired us and because we deal with an emotional genre. As a young Christian I would pray when I felt like it, witness when I felt like it, feel forgiven or feel condemned depending on my circumstances and mood. How do we get past those feelings?

God has given us His Word to be that instrument panel. "Sanctify them [us] in the truth," Jesus asked the Father. "Your word is truth" (John 17:17 ESV). God's Word can save us from crashing and burning in our Christian lives. But we do crash and burn, even those of us who know a lot about God's Word. Do we need something more?

If God's purpose is to make us like Christ, what did *Christ* need while living here on earth? Was Jesus able to work miracles because He is the Son of God, or because He is the Son of Man?

When Jesus walked this earth, He healed countless men and women. He touched people who had been crippled their entire life and suddenly they were able to walk, to dance, to run and jump. He opened the eyes of people who had never been able to see before, and they saw their first sunset, they looked into the eyes of their children for the first time.

Did Jesus do this because He is God?

Of course, Jesus must have been able to walk on water because He is the Son of God. But wait. Didn't someone else walk on water too? That's right, Peter walked on water. Okay, his walk was a short one, but even a short walk on water is fairly astonishing, wouldn't you say?

How did Peter do it? The same way that Jesus did it.

Listen to how Jesus explains it after rescuing Peter when Peter began to sink: "You of little faith . . . why did you doubt?" (Matthew 14:31). Peter walked on water by faith in God. He stopped walking on water when he started trusting his "gifting" and took his eyes off Jesus—and he got smacked in the mouth by a fistful of waves.

So how did Jesus walk on water? *By faith in God the Father.*

Notice something in a story Luke tells about one of the times Jesus was teaching. I skipped over it for years. It's the end of verse 17 in chapter 5. Luke, inspired by the Holy Spirit, pens these words: "And the power of the Lord was present for him to heal the sick."

Did you see it?

Me neither, until one day I asked myself, *Why did Luke say that? Isn't it obvious that the power of the Lord was present? Jesus was present! And if Jesus is present, the power of the Lord to heal is present too, right?*

And the thought occurred to me, *Maybe not.* After all, if it is always assumed that where Jesus is, the power is, then there is no need to mention it here. Luke doesn't say, "Jesus was breathing that day," or, "Jesus was wearing His clothes that day." No need to state the obvious.

So what is your point, Luke?

Jesus was dependent on the Father to give Him the power to heal, and sometimes the Father gave it, and sometimes He didn't. (Which creates a problem for the "name it, claim it" theology, which is polluting the landscape here in the young churches of Ukraine.)

Every miracle Jesus performed, He did so by faith in God the Father. Every healing, every casting out of demons, every feeding of thousands was done not because Jesus is the Son of God—which He is—but because Jesus was the Son of Man, totally dependent on the Father. Jesus spoke only things His Father told him, performed miracles only after asking for His Father's power. Every temptation Jesus faced (see Hebrews 4:15), He resisted, not because He is God, but because He had faith in God the Father.

Why is this important? If Jesus resisted temptation as God, what comfort is that to me? I'm not God. But if He resisted temptation by faith, then I too can resist temptation by faith. We both have access to the same faith and the same Father. Hallelujah!

◊ ◊ ◊

If you don't believe this yet, look at Acts 2:22: "Jesus of Nazareth, a man attested to you by God with mighty works and wonders and signs that God did through him" (ESV). Who did the miracles, wonders, and signs? God did, through Jesus!

This is why Jesus could say to us in John 14:12, "Truly, truly I say to you, whoever believes in me will also do the works that I do; and greater works than these will he do" (ESV).

You and I have read these verses and just shook our heads in disbelief. *I'm not God. How can I do the same things Jesus did?*

But this is not about us, our strength, our gifting. This is about the One and Only, God. Only He can do these things. Even our faith is a gift from Him. Hebrews 12 tells us Jesus is the author and perfecter of our faith. He begins and grows whatever faith I have, to His glory, not mine. It's all about the One.

Look at another example in Luke 5: So many people fill up the room where Jesus is that when some men bring a paralytic friend for healing, they are unable to get inside. You know the rest of the story. The men climb up on top of the house and lower their friend down through the tiles to Jesus.

"When Jesus saw their faith, he said, 'Friend, your sins are forgiven'" (Luke 5:20).

Forgiveness of sins can only be done by God. Even the Pharisees knew that. That's why they accused Jesus of blasphemy after He said this.

Jesus never stopped being God even though He put on flesh and bones for a season. But that is not what Jesus appeals to when He defends His offer of forgiveness. No, instead He says, "The Son of Man has *authority* on earth to forgive sins" (Luke 5:24). He could have said, "I am God and I can forgive sins." It was true. But Jesus laid aside His rights as God and took on the form of a servant (see Philippians 2:6–7).

Jesus talks about this authority in Matthew 28: "All authority in heaven and on earth has been *given* to me" (v. 18). Where did the Son of Man get His authority? From God the Father.

◊ ◊ ◊

Vertigo happens to us when we assume responsibility for flying in this dark place. When I submit to God's authority by trusting His word, I don't have to crash and burn every time temptation comes. Let's look at one last example of this authority.

In Luke 7, we read about a centurion whose valued servant is paralyzed and near death. This centurion had God's heart of compassion. He gave money to build the local synagogue. "He loves our nation," the Jewish leaders told Jesus (v. 5). And we see his tender heart as he asked for Jesus to heal his servant.

But just as Jesus approaches the man's home, servants are sent out to ask Jesus not to enter. The centurion says he is not worthy to have Jesus enter his home. "But say the word and my servant will be healed. For I myself am a man under authority, with soldiers under me. I tell this one, 'Go,' and he goes; and that one, 'Come,' and he comes. I say to my servant, 'Do this,' and he does it" (vv. 7–8).

Why do you suppose the centurion didn't say, "I too am a man *with* authority"? After all, wouldn't it be true? And wouldn't the parallel still stand regarding Jesus, for he, too, is a man *with* authority? But this man knew his own authority was delegated to him by Rome, and he seemed to understand that Jesus' authority was delegated by heaven. He knew Jesus only healed as the Father healed through him.

When Jesus sees this, He says something we only hear

from Him one other time in Scripture. Jesus was astonished at his faith (see v. 9). What was the other time Jesus was astonished? He was astonished at the unbelief of the people in His hometown of Nazareth. So we see Jesus astonished by the presence of faith and by the absence of faith.

The Son of Man is living by faith.

And now Jesus says to us, "All authority in heaven and earth has been given to me. Therefore go and make disciples of all nations. . . . And surely I am with you always, to the very end of the age" (Matthew 28:18–20).

Where does our authority come from? From Jesus, who gets it from the Father. And our comfort is found in knowing that Jesus is with us—always.

So having and knowing God's Word isn't enough to keep us from crashing. We must *believe* it.

Jesus didn't say, "If you know these things, blessed are you." He said, "If you know these things, blessed are you if you 'do' them" (see Luke 11:28).

Yet when He was asked, "What must we do, to be doing the works of God?" (John 6:28 ESV). Jesus answered, "Believe" (6:29 ESV).

◊ ◊ ◊

Let me pull the thoughts of this chapter together by asking a question: Whose reputation is on the line when we submit to God's authority by trusting His word?

God's reputation, of course. This problem of vertigo— the confusion in my thoughts and emotions—is normal for people of the dark. No wonder building my own reputation is so unsatisfying. It's faith in God and His word that quiets the voices in my head. When I believe in His authority, I am not putting my name at stake but God's name.

We have said that who we are in Christ is the truest thing about us. Will we believe?

◊ ◊ ◊

But there is more, much more. Have you ever been surf fishing on Haystack Rock? . . .

space

"Everything that is life, and good, everything that is beautiful, delicious, and compelling, alive forever within the One!"

sk Westerners, "Who are you?" and they will answer with their head. "We think, therefore we are." Some might quote Solomon: "As [a man] thinks in his heart, so is he" (Proverbs 23:7 NKJV). But what is the difference between *thinking* and thinking in your heart? Are they the same?

In the "great commandment" God commanded us to "Love the Lord your God with all your heart and with all your soul and with all your mind and with all your strength" (Mark 12:30). We in the West have focused on loving God with all our heart, mind, and strength. But we have not always figured out the "soul" part so well. We pride ourselves on our exegesis. Our evangelical sermons are didactic to a fault. We are strong in our apologetics whether debating the bio un-ethics of cloning human beings or arguing for moral absolutes in our postmodern schools. And the mind is fully engaged.

Ask our brothers and sisters in eastern Europe, "Who are you?" and they will answer with their souls. And this may be closer to what Solomon had in mind. Our Slavic friends have much to teach us. It is no surprise that they have a depth in literature and art that much of the world can only dream about—if we still dream at all.

◊ ◊ ◊

Plato said, "If man is anything at all, he is soul." In the soul, God manifests Himself in the richest, most intimate ways.

He restores not my mind but my soul. He leads me in the paths of righteousness for His name's sake, David sings in the beautiful Twenty-Third Psalm (v. 3, my paraphrase). And in Psalm 42, *As the deer pants for flowing streams, so pants my soul [not mind, not body] for You, oh God. My soul thirsts for God, for the living God* (vv. 1–2).

The psalmist asks twice in Psalm 42, "Why are you cast down, O my soul, and why are you in turmoil within me?" (v. 11 ESV). It isn't thoughts that are confused—although of course that may be true too. But as the Holy Spirit inspires these words, He places a magnifying glass over our soul and invites us to take a look.

The psalmist also writes, "I remember . . . how I would go with the throng and lead them in the procession to the house of God with glad shouts and songs of praise" (Psalm 42:4 ESV). He remembers the real presence of God; he remembers the joy of celebrating and praising the living God. He remembers their relationship.

This kind of remembering begins not in the memory, not in the mind, but in the uncharted territory of the soul. The soul is a deeper place than thoughts or actions—it is where my will is shaped. What a surprise—I thought my will was determined by my mind.

But I have much information recorded in my thoughts that I never act on. I know what to do but do something else. Why is this? Perhaps because my will—my choice maker—is some place else, in my soul. Only when I come to God with my soul as well as my intellect will I discover more of Him. And the One who made us in His image longs for that soul intimacy.

If our soul is the place we meet with God, why is it so foreign to us? It is impossible for us to dissect a human being and isolate the soul—we cannot easily separate soul from thought from action. But God can. The writer of Hebrews tells us, "The word of God is living and active, sharper than any two-edged sword, piercing to the division of soul and of spirit, of joints and of marrow, and discerning the thoughts and intentions of the heart" (4:12 ESV).

And this is why we are often afraid of our soul—we cannot control it, we cannot make it do what we want it to. We cannot manipulate it as we try to influence the opinions of others; we cannot show off in front of it as we strive to impress. Yet in it we find a reflection of who we are, the ultimate answer to, *What is the truest thing about me?* Only in our honest repentance can we find a deeper intimacy with our Soul-giver, the One.

The soul is the last frontier. This is where we explore in order to discover more about our great God. The soul shows us as clearly as our intellect and strength the *imago Dei* in us, the beauty of the One.

◊ ◊ ◊

But how do we get to God through our soul?

As a music professor, one of the courses I taught was composition—how to write music. Beginning songwriters are as easy to spot as beginning eaters. They take both hands and grab for anything and everything in front of them and begin to stuff it in their mouths. New songwriters reach for every chord they know, mix it with every colorful cliché they can steal, and add crumbs of inspiration for texture. What a song. What a mess.

Christians who are beginning songwriters can be even messier, often adding everything from Genesis to Revelation for fear of leaving out some important doctrine and opening themselves to charges of heresy.

So one of the first points I wanted to teach my young writers was this: You must create space in your songs.

We create space with "rests," word pictures, and repetition. We simplify some melodies or chord progressions, sacrificing the opportunity to show everything we know on the altar of writing one good song. Space gives the listener a chance to feel, to own and respond to the music. Space allows the listener the opportunity to become part of the song.

This principle is true for authors as well. Start with me. How does this book create space for you to respond? How do these thoughts leave space for you to process them? Do the stories create the space necessary for your soul to be engaged?

When God graciously allowed our family to move to Ukraine and work with "creatives" there, it became obvious that my communication style was in for a face-lift. I love words. I fill up journals with words, write lyrics for musicals, write articles for magazines, and now I am writing a book. God must have been laughing when He sent me to a country where my words would only be noise to 90 percent of the country.

Perhaps He sent me because I needed space to meet Him in my soul. Perhaps I needed to understand more of His saving grace. Because space, as God defines it, is a means of salvation.

When I was in seminary, I was fascinated by a Hebrew professor's definition of the word *salvation*. The original context of this word had to do with living conditions in Israel. Small rooms cramped up against other small rooms with low ceilings, dirt floors, and tiny windows. Some of you are already feeling claustrophobic.

Dr. Ronald Allen told us, "Salvation means, 'room to breathe.'"

Isn't that great? Room to breathe—when my world is collapsing all around me, dust is flying, and people are pushing and shoving, I need room to breathe. I need salvation. When your thoughts are scrambled and voices assault you, you need room to breathe. This is salvation. This is space! We are not saved to be independent from God. God has given us salvation so that we can find Him. He offers us this salvation—this space—so we can meet Him on a soul-level, beyond the words and accusations and fears and rumblings of our minds. And He offers us this space in a host of creative ways.

◊ ◊ ◊

One example of space God has written into our lives is a need He created within us. It is the need for sleep. This is the body's equivalent of sustained high-arching phrases in music and empty stretches of canvas in an oil painting. This is "room to breathe" for the body. When we sleep, we are enjoying God's design of space in the human life cycle.

Now think about physical creation. God has created

mountains and valleys, forests and deserts. He has splattered the midnight sky with stars and dared us to count them all. Space within space. The beauty He offers gives us room to breathe.

The space of God's creation struck me again several years ago when I was fishing with a friend of mine in Portland, Oregon. This friend was a professional fishing guide and on this occasion we were balancing precariously on Haystack Rock—on the coastline of the Pacific's Cannon Beach. (If you ever saw an early Steven Spielberg movie, *Goonies*, this was the setting of the last scene when the old pirate ship is discovered and set free to float away.)

So my friend and I ran into a school of ocean trout and we were each catching them three at a time. What a rush!

That night I was cleaning fish and I grasped this slippery, stunning, black-and-orange trout and slit it open. To my surprise the flesh inside was a beautiful turquoise. And it struck me—the extravagance of God's design and creation.

God painted dramatic lines of black and orange and then hidden inside He splashed vivid turquoise. Having meticulously designed this fish, He put it in the bottom of the ocean where no eye would see it. No camera would capture it and no artist would paint it.

Can you believe such a waste of creation? But this was not a waste at all. The One enjoyed watching it, and it is a wonderful picture of the extravagance of our Creator God. Multiply this one fish by millions and then add the coral flowers and the shells of exquisite design all drowning in oceans of saltwater, and we are swimming in God's common grace.

God has given His creation room to breathe. And in this space our soul finds God! Our soul sings and paints and

writes and reflects and worships God! And God is extrava-
gant beyond words and it's good and it's right to stare in
awe, to be silenced by the grandeur of our God. In this
space called creation, our soul recognizes God. We are
surprised and delighted with a creativity that transcends
mere words, a creativity that reminds us we are more than
the sum of our parts—we were made for eternal things.

And the fly fisherman stands knee deep in a beautiful
ice-cold mountain stream and laughs and cries with delight
over the wonder of such beauty. In this place without walls
and pews, his soul knows there is a God and if he refuses to
worship the One, the mountains and trout stand in judgment against him.

Allow the vast melodies of a symphony to carry you to
the throne of God. Paint abstract oils, knowing that God is
revealing Himself in the vivid reds and blues, hiding again
in the shadows of a still life, and shouting down from
Michelangelo's Sistine Chapel, "I'm still touching
humankind!"

◊ ◊ ◊

Our story began with an eighteen-year-old violinist fail-
ing spectacularly in his performance.

My own inconvenient conception begged the question,
"How does this unwanted child believe he is loved?"

And Billy Batson taught us that we are all, in some way,
looking for the truth about who and why we are, and some
of us are discovering our need for a Savior. But gradually as
we looked at our darkness and our desire for fairness, we
realized we've made life to be all about us. We who are
children of God have pretended that we are still orphans.

The One patiently and powerfully reminds us that the

truest thing about us is wonderfully swallowed up in the truth about Him. He invites us to seek Him. To repent profoundly. "Be still," God says, "and know that I am God" (Psalm 46:10). And I want to ask, "Is that it?" After all these pages and thoughts and stories is this how we end? "Be still and know"?

And I think of the little girl, born in the heart of the Great Depression. She was only fifty-six years old when cancer overwhelmed her and she went home to be with the Jesus she had given her heart to.

I'll never forget the moment I stood by the hospital bed looking at this strong woman who wanted—more than any person I'd ever known—to please Jesus. She had breathed her last breath. Dad stood between my brother, Steve, and me, his arms around us, and through his tears he said, "Boys, never forget. Never forget that God is good." Do you see the scene? A recovering alcoholic father, a weeping son who is still struggling with anger, and my younger brother looking at a mother who's once again a little girl in the arms of her heavenly Father. And it is the broken and forgiven dad who leads us to Jesus. Be still—cease striving. In this space, in this darkness, be still and know that the One is God. And God is still good.

◊ ◊ ◊

We have looked in the wrong places to find out the truest thing about us. When we finally look into the eyes of the One, we are at once defined and forgotten, and it is as it should be.

The only reputation that matters, the only reputation that ever mattered, is the reputation of God, the Three in One. "Therefore God exalted him to the highest place and gave him the name that is above every name" (Philippians 2:9). He who is "the radiance of God's glory and the exact representation of his being" (Hebrews 1:3).

The only name worth dropping is worshiped. "That at the name of Jesus, every knee should bow . . . and every tongue confess that Jesus Christ is Lord, to the glory of God the Father" (Philippians 2:10–11).

All creation is at once embarrassed and silenced by its own glory in light of the wonder of Jesus. And suddenly creation explodes in worship, and it's only the beginning. . . .

notes

1. A. Skevington Wood in *The Expositor's Bible Commentary*, Frank E. Gaebelein, ed. (Grand Rapids, MI: Zondervan, 1982), 62.

about the author

Paul Thorson and his wife, Gail, are planting a church (Bozhy Dotyk) in Kiev, Ukraine, where they serve in a community of artists and musicians. Paul speaks at conferences worldwide with various organizations and also regularly preaches in churches throughout Ukraine. With a bachelor's degree in music performance and a master's degree in church music, he was on staff with Campus Crusade for Christ for nearly thirteen years, traveling as a solo artist. He has also been an associate professor of music at Colorado Christian University and Belmont University, a writer for *CCM* magazine and a longtime Bible teacher at Christ Community Church in Franklin, Tennessee. Paul and Gail are currently with World Harvest Mission.